20 '81

D0462687

THE BATTLE OF
MIDWAY

THE BATTLE OF
MIDWAY

IRA PECK

SCHOLASTIC BOOK SERVICES
New York Toronto London Auckland Sydney

ISBN: 0-590-01437-4

12 11 10 9   9/7 0 1/8

Printed in the U.S.A.

CONTENTS

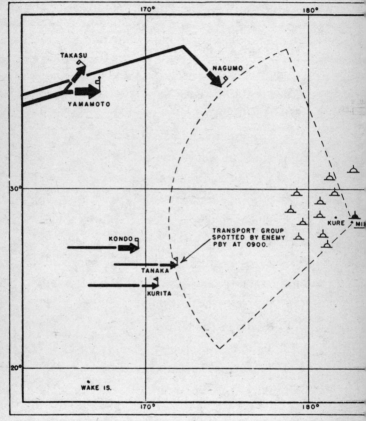

Disposition of U.S. and Japanese naval forces in Midway area,

From *Midway: The Battle That Doomed Japan* by Mitsuo Fuchida and Masatake Okumiya. Copyright © 1955, United States Naval Institute.

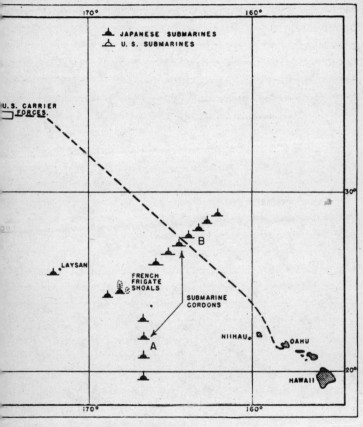

June 3, 1942. Carriers battled next day.

I

MIDWAY—THE TURNING POINT

The news from the Pacific could not have been worse in the months following the Japanese attack on Pearl Harbor, December 7, 1941. Within hours of the devastation wreaked on the U.S. warships and planes in Hawaii, Japanese armed forces launched a vast campaign of conquest in southeast Asia and the Pacific. The swiftness of their advances stunned the United States and its allies, and probably surprised even the Japanese. Almost every week, newspaper headlines told of another spectacular Japanese victory, another American, British, or Dutch disaster. Guam, Wake Island, Hong Kong, Manila, Malaya, Singapore, the Netherlands East Indies, and Burma fell to the Japanese invaders in rapid succession. On May 6, 1942, Corregidor, the last U.S. stronghold in the Philippines, surrendered after prolonged and heroic resistance. The American public was plunged into gloom.

At this date, the Japanese had attained practically all the objectives they had set for themselves initially, and with a minimum of losses. They were masters of a huge empire in Asia, and their navy dominated the seas from the western Pacific to the Indian Ocean. Under the circumstances, the Japanese might have been expected to take a deep breath before attempting any further aggressive moves. Instead, they hastily assembled the largest and most powerful naval force in history to strike yet another blow. Its objective hardly seemed to be worth such an enormous effort: Midway Atoll, a tiny U.S. base in the Pacific about 2,000 miles from Japan. What was the importance of Midway to the Japanese? Strategically, its value was very limited. The entire atoll consists of two islets, Sand and Eastern, separated by a lagoon and comprising about two square miles. Midway's great distance from Japan made it difficult to supply. Its relative proximity to Pearl Harbor made it vulnerable to American counterattacks. Why risk a huge naval force for such a dubious objective?

The answer goes back to the events of December 7, 1941. The Japanese attack on Pearl Harbor had sunk or badly damaged every battleship in the U.S. Pacific Fleet, as well as a number of other ships. By a stroke of good fortune, however, all three of our Pacific Fleet aircraft carriers were at sea that morning and so were unscathed. Since then, they had carried out several hit-and-run strikes against Japanese bases in the Pacific, and one spectacular raid against Tokyo itself. Although these strikes inflicted relatively minor damage, they convinced Japan's military leaders that their empire would not be secure until the menace of these prowling aircraft carriers was removed. The Tokyo raid was especially galling, for it had endangered the life of Emperor Hirohito.

Admiral Isoroku Yamamoto, the Commander in Chief of the Japanese Navy, was determined to engage the U.S. carriers in action and destroy them. He was sure that an attack on Midway would lure the U.S. Pacific Fleet into battle, and with his much larger forces, the odds would be all in his favor. So Midway was really the bait to draw the carriers, now the main strength of the U.S. Pacific Fleet, into a direct confrontation with the Japanese Navy. The capture of Midway to use as a base was only secondary.

Yamamoto was correct in assuming that an attack on Midway would be resisted by the U.S. Navy with all the means at its disposal. But the outcome of the battle was anything but what he had expected. By a combination of remarkable courage, determination, and opportunism, the U.S. Pacific Fleet won a smashing victory and thereby turned the tide of war against Japan. Although the Japanese Navy still remained a formidable force, after Midway it was reduced to a defensive role. Now it was America's turn to take the offensive, and this it did unrelentingly until final victory was won.

II

A PROGRAM OF CONQUEST

The war that began so suddenly when Japanese bombs and torpedoes devastated Pearl Harbor, Hawaii, had been coming for a long time. It was considered "inevitable" by some people as far back as 1898 when the United States acquired the Philippine Islands from Spain and became a power in the Far East. At this time, Japan was also becoming a major power in the Far East. Her immediate ambition was to control the ancient kingdom of Korea and the Chinese region of Manchuria. Her chief rival for domination of these areas was Czarist Russia. In 1904, the Japanese attacked the Russian fleet based at Port Arthur, Manchuria, and in the ensuing war thoroughly trounced her European rival. As a result, Japan gained control of Korea and became the dominant economic power in Manchuria. Japan extended her power in World War I by siding with the Allies against Germany. With a minimum of effort, Japan acquired Germany's island empire in the Pacific — the Marshall and Caroline Islands, and all the Marianas except Guam, which was a U.S. possession. Now Japan and the United States were the chief rivals for supremacy in the Pacific.

Both American and Japanese naval strategists were already thinking in terms of a future war between their two countries. From 1918 on, future Japanese Navy officers were indoctrinated with the idea that "the potential enemy is America." The Japanese Navy was committed to a "southward advance" — the Philippines — which they knew would provoke a war with the United States. Conceding the superior strength of the U.S., Japanese Navy planners developed a defensive strategy: The role of the Imperial Navy would be to intercept and attack the U.S. fleet in waters close to the Japanese homeland. Accordingly, Japanese warships were designed to assure them every possible advantage in such an encounter.

Anticipating a possible seizure of the Philippines by Japan, U.S. Navy officers drew up their own plans for such a contingency. Our Navy's "Orange" plan called for the U.S. Army to defend Manila, holding out long enough for the fleet to cross the Pacific and raise the siege.

While naval strategists were making plans for a possible war, political leaders in the United States, Great Britain, Japan, and other countries were exploring the possibilities of peace. After the terrible slaughter unleashed during World

War I, popular sentiment in most countries was strongly anti-militaristic. Disarmament soon became the order of the day. In 1921, the leading naval powers met in Washington, D.C., to discuss limiting both the number and size of their warships. The Washington Conference produced a treaty that effectively restricted the size of naval forces for the next 15 years. One of its chief provisions created a 5:5:3 ratio in battleship and carrier tonnage that applied to the United States (5), Great Britain (5), and Japan (3). Although ardent Japanese nationalists protested that the agreement was designed to keep their country "inferior," in the long run it benefited Japan. It enabled her to become the strongest naval power in the Pacific, for the United States had two oceans to defend, and Great Britain had three. In 1936, when militarists were in almost complete control of the country, Japan announced that it would not renew the naval limitations agreement and began a full-scale build-up of its Navy. By 1941, the Japanese Navy was more powerful than the combined U.S. and British fleets in the Pacific, and in a much better state of combat readiness.

The assumption of power by Japan's militarists in the 1930's paralleled Adolf Hitler's rise to power in Germany and was motivated by a similar ambition — world conquest. The Army had long enjoyed a favored position in Japanese society. It was, in fact, more representative of the nation and its aspirations than the liberal, pro-Western civilians who temporarily ruled Japan in the 1920's. Japan's ancient religious and social traditions exalted the military profession and regarded war and conquest as the highest good. These traditions were still very strong in the 20th century, however much Japan had changed in other ways. The Japanese were proud to serve in the armed forces and quite willing to die for their Emperor. Then, they believed, they would become demigods or spirits and guard their native land.

Thwarted by liberal, parliamentary rule in the 1920's, Japan's militarists resorted to a campaign of harassment and terror against civilian officials. They organized a political movement called Kodo-Ha, which was similar to Hitler's Nazi movement in Germany. Kodo-Ha aimed to put Japan under Army rule, and to place all the Far East under Japanese domination. This, in turn, would lead to *Hakko Ichiu* — "bringing the eight corners of the world under one roof." It was, in short, a program for the conquest and subjugation of all the world by Japan.

Japan's militarists struck their first blow in September, 1931. Although Japan already dominated Manchuria economically, it now sought to annex the region completely. Accordingly, Japanese agents exploded a bomb on the tracks of the South Manchurian Railroad, and a Japanese army based in Korea quickly moved in to "restore order." This created a state of war with China, which enabled the militarists to assume control of the Japanese government. Meanwhile, both the United States and the League of Nations, a peace-keeping organization similar to today's United Nations, condemned Japan's annexation of Manchuria. Japan's answer was to withdraw from the League, and later to announce that it would no longer be bound by naval limitations agreements.

By 1937, Japan's militarists were ready for a second round of war with China. This time, a Japanese army supposedly on "training maneuvers" in north China provoked a clash with Chinese troops near Peking and began a carefully planned campaign of conquest. In December, the Japanese captured Nanking, China's capital at the time. For several days, the conquerors raped and slaughtered its inhabitants and committed wholesale destruction.

Japan's conquests in China were making her military leaders increasingly arrogant. Just before the Japanese entered Nanking, officials of the American Embassy prepared to leave the city on a small U.S. naval vessel, the gunboat *Panay*. The *Panay* was one of five gunboats that patrolled the Yangtze river to protect U.S. citizens and commerce against Chinese guerrilla bands. The *Panay* embarked on December 11, and the next day was anchored upstream from Nanking. It was a bright, sunny day, and the gunboat was clearly identified by American flags. Suddenly it was attacked from the air by about 15 Japanese bombers and nine fighter planes. The crew of the *Panay* fought back with .30-calibre machine guns, but several bomb hits soon sent the gunboat to the bottom. As the survivors rowed to shore, they were repeatedly strafed by the fighter planes. Two sailors and one civilian were killed in the attack and 12 others were seriously wounded.

The Japanese government hastened to apologize, explaining that the attack had been a mistake — the pilots thought the *Panay* was a Chinese vessel. A U.S. Naval Court of Inquiry produced substantial evidence that the attack was deliberate, and no mistake. But the United States government was so anxious to avoid war that it accepted the Japanese explanation and the offer of an indemnity. The American people seemed to approve the decision. A public opinion poll indicated that 70 percent of the people favored a complete withdrawal of all U.S. civilians and armed forces from China.

What was the United States doing to counter the threat of Japanese aggression and a rapidly expanding Imperial Navy? From 1920 to 1933, very little was done at all. According to Fleet Admiral Ernest J. King, "Except for cruisers, hardly any combatant ships (no battleships or destroyers) were added to our own fleet during that period and few were under construction...." Then, in 1933, Franklin D. Roosevelt, who had been Assistant Secretary of the Navy during World War I, became President of the United States. Almost immediately, the first new construction of Navy ships in years was authorized, ostensibly to help alleviate the widespread unemployment that existed during the Depression. Among the ships laid down were two aircraft carriers, the *Enterprise* and the *Yorktown*. These ships, as we shall see, were two of the three carriers that turned back the Japanese at the Battle of Midway. The third U.S. aircraft carrier that took part in the action, the *Hornet*, was laid down in 1939. By 1941, the U.S. Navy had added about 218,000 tons to its 1922 total of 1.1 million tons. By contrast, the Japanese had almost doubled their 1922 total of 547,000 tons. When the Japanese struck at Pearl Harbor, the U.S. Navy was in the unenviable position of having to fight a two-ocean war with less than a one-ocean fleet.

III

JAPAN CHOOSES WAR

The outbreak of World War II in Europe, September 1, 1939, created new opportunities for Japan's militarist leaders in the Far East. While Adolf Hitler's armies were threatening Europe, Japan felt strong enough to proclaim her own territorial ambitions in Asia. Her grand design was the establishment of a "Greater East Asia Co-Prosperity Sphere." It meant Japanese domination of Indochina, Malaya, Burma, the Philippines, and the Netherlands East Indies as well as China. In May-June of 1940, German armies crushed Holland and France, and left England fighting for its very survival. The coveted Far Eastern empires of these countries now looked like easy pickings to Japan's war lords. Only the United States could stand in the way of their conquest. So far, the United States had done little more than issue futile diplomatic protests against Japanese aggression. Meanwhile, the Japanese were buying huge quantities of iron, steel, and oil in the U.S. that were essential to keep their war machine going. Why didn't the U.S. government cut off this trade with Japan? It feared that to do so would stimulate further Japanese aggression to obtain raw materials elsewhere and possibly provoke war.

By the summer of 1940, it was apparent that the policy of appeasing Japan was a self-defeating one for the United States. In July, Congress authorized President Roosevelt to prohibit or curtail the export of war materials whenever he deemed it "necessary in the interest of national defense." President Roosevelt quickly began to impose embargoes on the sale of many strategic war materials to Japan.

Japan's answer was to sign a formal treaty of alliance in September with Europe's Axis powers, Germany and Italy. Japan and Nazi Germany had been drawing closer together for some time. Their political philosophies were similar, and now they saw a military advantage in a pledge of mutual cooperation. By the terms of the Tripartite Pact, Japan's war lords recognized Hitler's "New Order in Europe." Germany and Italy, in turn, recognized "the leadership of Japan in the establishment of a New Order in Greater East Asia." The three partners pledged to assist each other if "attacked by a power not involved in the European war or in the Sino-Japanese conflict." This, of course, clearly meant the United States.

Japan's appetite for a "southward advance" was now whetted. If the United States tried to interfere, it would have to contend with Germany and Italy as well as Japan.

Even before the pact was signed, Japan's militarists were profiting from their good relations with Nazi Germany. Late in August, Japanese troops invaded northern Indochina, which was then part of the French empire. Hitler persuaded the puppet French government at Vichy to accept the Japanese occupation. Gradually, the Japanese extended their occupation to all of Indochina.

The United States was seriously alarmed by Japan's move into Indochina. It was the first breach of the status quo in the Far East since the beginning of World War II. When Japan took over Indochina completely in July, 1941, President Roosevelt responded emphatically. He issued an order that effectively shut off all trade between Japan and the United States, including the immense quantities of oil that were still being shipped to Japan.

The embargo on oil hit the Japanese militarists particularly hard, since Japan imported most of its oil from the United States. Without it, Japanese industry and the armed forces would grind to a halt within a year. Now the militarists were faced with a critical dilemma. To obtain American oil, they would have to renounce their plans for conquest. This they were loathe to do.

13

The other alternative was to launch their campaign of conquest soon, while they still had adequate reserves of oil. Once the East Indies were seized, they would have all the oil they needed. Confident that their armed forces would be successful, and that the United States would be crushed quickly, they chose the course of war.

President Roosevelt had taken other steps in the hope of deterring Japanese aggression. One of these was the decision to station the Pacific Fleet at Pearl Harbor, Hawaii, rather than at its usual West Coast bases. Admiral James O. Richardson, the Fleet's Commander in Chief, was disturbed by the switch, which he believed was strategically unsound. From Pearl Harbor, he queried Admiral H.R. Stark, Chief of Naval Operations in Washington, D.C., "Why are we here?" Stark's reply was, "You are there because of the deterrent effect which it is thought your presence may have on the Japs going into the East Indies." Later President Roosevelt told Richardson in a personal interview that the presence of the Fleet at Hawaii "has had and is now having a restraining influence on Japan."

The embargo on the sale of U.S. oil to Japan brought the tensions between the two countries to a head. Japan's military leaders secretly began drafting comprehensive war plans, while the United States accelerated its military preparations, including the construction of a two-ocean fleet.

As preparations for war were intensifying, Japanese and American diplomats in Washington, D.C., were conducting negotiations to avert war or, at least, to postpone it. The negotiators on both sides frequently proclaimed their desire for peace, and undoubtedly were sincere about it. The problem was that their conditions for peace were diametrically opposed. To the Japanese diplomats, peace hinged upon our willingness to accept Japanese domination of Greater East Asia. To the U.S. diplomats, peace hinged upon Japan's renunciation of this ambition and the evacuation of her military forces from China and Indochina. These positions were impossible to reconcile, and as a result the negotiations dragged on for months.

Meanwhile, unknown to either the Japanese or American negotiators, Japan's militarists were making some fateful decisions at home. In September, the Japanese Army prepared three resolutions that were approved by the Imperial Council presided over by Emperor Hirohito. The gist of these resolutions was that if the United States and England did not agree to Japan's demands soon, "We will immediately make up our minds to get ready for war against America and England and Holland." The deadline for meeting Japan's demands was later set at November 29, 1941. On November 26, a powerful Japanese Navy force was scheduled to leave home waters on a course bound for Hawaii. If the United

States did not give in to Japan's demands by November 29, the naval force would be signaled to proceed to Hawaii and carry out the mission for which it had been carefully trained—the destruction of the U.S. Pacific Fleet at Pearl Harbor.

IV

THE SECRET MISSION

Admiral Yamamoto, the Commander in Chief of the Japanese Combined Fleet, had never been eager for a war with the United States. Early in his career, he had served as a naval aide with the Japanese Embassy in Washington, D.C., and had acquired a healthy respect for America's industrial might. He knew that this country was capable of producing warships at a far greater rate than Japan. In the event of a war, it would not be long before the U.S. Fleet attained a preponderance in numbers. Consequently, he had opposed Japan's alliance with Germany and Italy, and the drift toward war with the United States. Just before the war, he was asked for an estimate of the Japanese Navy's chances in a conflict with the U.S. Fleet. His answer was, "If I am told to fight regardless of the consequence, I shall run wild considerably for the first six months or a year, but I have utterly no confidence for the second and third years."

For expressing such doubts, Yamamoto was

accused of cowardice by the Japanese Army, which was convinced of Japan's "invincibility." But once Japan's leaders decided upon war, Yamamoto put all his talents as a naval tactician to work to ensure his country's success. The basic war plan proposed by the Japanese Naval General Staff—the "desk admirals"—was essentially the same one favored by its strategists for at least two decades. The Japanese Navy would employ the bulk of its surface and air strength, including its carriers, in support of a thrust southward to seize the Philippines, Malaya, and the East Indies, the main objectives. Optimistically, this would be accomplished before the U.S. Pacific Fleet based far away at Pearl Harbor could interfere. (The Fleet would first have to clear out the Japanese bases in the Marshalls and Carolines, a job that would take many months.) If not, the Japanese Fleet would remain in home waters, and there intercept and destroy the U.S. Fleet when it came out to attack. This was in keeping with the old "defensive" doctrine of Japanese naval planners.

Admiral Yamamoto, however, had other ideas. Since January, 1941, he had been considering the possibilities of dealing a knockout blow to the U.S. Pacific Fleet at the very outset of the war. An aggressive champion of naval aviation, he had concluded that a surprise attack on Pearl Harbor by carrier aircraft was the answer.

When Yamamoto proposed his plan to the

Naval General Staff, it met with strong opposition. The diversion of a substantial part of the Fleet, including most of its carriers, to the Pearl Harbor attack would endanger the success of the "southward advance," Yamamoto's critics maintained. Furthermore, it was too much of a gamble. Its success depended on completely surprising the U.S. Fleet within its base. What if Pearl Harbor was alerted to the attack? The consequences to the Japanese force might be disastrous. Other critics pointed out the great vulnerability of carriers to air attacks.

Yamamoto, however, insisted upon his plan. Basically he believed that Japan's main chance for victory lay in destroying the U.S. Pacific Fleet before American industry could tip the scales hopelessly against his country. If the Fleet at Pearl Harbor was quickly wiped out, Japan would firmly control the western Pacific. Its empire could be developed and made so secure that no one would risk attacking it. Then the United States would *have* to sue for peace on Japan's terms. Yamamoto saw no reason to wait for the U.S. Pacific Fleet to arrive in Japan's home waters. With the aid of naval aviation, it could be destroyed in its own lair.

When the Naval General Staff still hesitated, Yamamoto threatened to resign. Rather than lose the services of Japan's foremost naval commander, the General Staff finally gave its consent to his plan. This was on November 3, just five weeks before the attack was actually delivered.

Meanwhile, Japanese aircraft carriers had already begun training for the attack in September, though the crews were not yet aware of their mission. Bombing was practiced at an isolated island in home waters, and special attention was given to the problem of dropping aerial torpedoes in shallow depths. Pearl Harbor was only about 40 feet deep, so the torpedoes had to be fitted with special fins that would keep them from hitting bottom.

On October 5, 100 aviators who were to take part in the attack were called to a meeting aboard the flagship carrier *Akagi*. There Admiral Yamamoto told them that they had been selected to destroy the U.S. Pacific Fleet at Hawaii on or about December 8. (This was the Japanese calendar date. In Hawaii, it would be December 7.) Admiral Yamamoto chose that day because it would be a Sunday, and he knew that most of the Pacific Fleet was brought into Pearl Harbor every weekend. Yamamoto urged his aviators to hit hard. He assured them that the United States would be unable to recover in time to prevent Japan from seizing Southeast Asia. For the time being, the aviators were sworn to keep their mission a secret.

While these secret preparations were taking place in Japan, the "peace" negotiations in Washington, D.C., were grinding on. On October 18, General Hideki Tojo, an ardent Kodo-Ha militarist, became Premier of Japan and began to press his negotiators in Washington to come to an agreement with the United States by the end of November. Tojo's "absolutely final proposal" for peace was delivered in Washington on November 20. It was basically the same proposal that our diplomats had been rejecting all along, and offered no real possibility for peace.

That Japan was actively preparing to wage war was no secret to President Roosevelt and his advisers. For some time, U.S. intelligence units had been intercepting and decoding the Japanese government's radio messages to its embassy in Washington. The President and his advisers knew that Tojo's deadline for acceptance of his proposal was November 29. They also knew that Japanese armed forces were poised to strike if the proposal was not accepted. The only question was, where? By November 25, Army and Navy intelligence units had evidence of Japanese ship and troop movements to the south. But so far there had been no hint of the existence of a carrier force set to strike at Pearl Harbor.

On November 26, according to plan, the Pearl Harbor Striking Force set out from an isolated and desolate bay on one of Japan's northern Kurile Islands. Commanded by Rear Admiral Chuichi Nagumo, it was centered on six big aircraft carriers. They were the 36,500-ton *Akagi* and the 38,200-ton *Kaga*, both of them larger than any U.S. aircraft carrier at that time; the

Shokaku and *Zuikaku*, each about 26,000 tons and quite new, having just gone into service in August; the *Hiryu* and *Soryu*, each about 17,500 tons. Together these warships carried 423 planes. Of them, 353 were assigned to execute the strike at Pearl Harbor. They included about 100 "Kates" equipped for high-level bombing; 40 Kates equipped for low-level torpedo-bombing; 131 "Val" dive bombers; and 79 Zero fighters, also known as "Zekes." (The rather quaint nicknames of these Japanese planes were bestowed on them by U.S. servicemen for easy identification purposes.)

The six carriers steamed toward Hawaii in two columns, with a battleship at the rear of each, two destroyers on the left, and three submarines on the right. A heavy cruiser patrolled either side from a distance of several miles, while other destroyers steamed ahead on the look-out for ships. Their orders were to shoot on sight any American, British, or Dutch merchant ships they might encounter. However, the Striking Force had deliberately chosen a stormy, northern route to reduce the possibility of meeting any shipping. It saw only one vessel on the way, and it turned out to be Japanese. As expected, the Striking Force ran into gale winds and heavy seas. Men were swept overboard, pennants torn to shreds, and the job of refueling from tankers was accomplished only with great difficulty. Meanwhile the Japanese pilots continued to study maps and photographs of Pearl Harbor and other targets in

Hawaii until they knew them better than any native Hawaiians.

As December 2 began, Admiral Nagumo had not yet received the radio message he was expecting from Admiral Yamamoto in Japan. This message would tell him whether he was to proceed with the attack on Pearl Harbor, or turn back. The decision, of course, rested upon the outcome of the negotiations in Washington. A cautious man who had opposed the Pearl Harbor plan when it was first proposed, Nagumo would have welcomed an order to turn back. However, it was not to be. On December 1, the Japanese government approved Tojo's decision to go to war. The next day, Nagumo received a three-word code message from Yamamoto: *Climb Mount Niitaka.* It meant that he was to carry out the attack on Pearl Harbor. The crews of the Japanese warships were then informed of their destination for the first time. The announcement was greeted with considerable enthusiasm. The Japanese had been fed a steady diet of anti-American propaganda by their leaders. Now these sailors saw a chance to strike a blow at the hated enemy. Few, if any, seemed troubled about the fact that they were about to wreak slaughter upon American sailors, soldiers, and civilians without any warning at all.

On December 6, Admiral Nagumo received the latest intelligence reports from Tokyo on the number and type of ships present at Pearl Harbor. In one respect, these reports were very disturbing. They indicated that no U.S. carriers were in port. The Japanese had fully expected to find three, or possibly four, carriers at Pearl Harbor, and these had been given top priority as targets. (Naval leaders on both sides were beginning to sense that carriers, not battleships, would be the mainstays of fleet actions in World War II.) Despite the absence of the carriers, Admiral Nagumo and his staff decided to carry out the attack as planned.

That evening, the Striking Force reached a point about 490 miles north of Oahu, the Hawaiian island on which Pearl Harbor and adjacent Honolulu are located. The carrier crews were assembled on the flight decks, and fervid, patriotic speeches were delivered by the air commanders. A high pitch of emotion was reached when the flag of Japan's greatest naval hero in the Russo-Japanese War, Admiral Togo, was raised aloft. Through the rest of the night, the Striking Force steamed southward toward Oahu. Before dawn, Admiral Nagumo reached the position he had chosen to launch his carrier planes, about 275 miles north of Pearl Harbor. At 6 A.M., the carriers began to launch the first wave of attack planes, 183 in all.

Excitement was high, and cheers of *banzai!* accompanied each plane as it took off. The planes circled overhead waiting for the signal from their commander, Captain Mitsuo Fuchida, to proceed.

Then they sped toward their target, which would soon be illuminated by a brilliant morning sunrise. At about 7:40, Fuchida spotted Oahu, and within minutes was in sight of Pearl Harbor on the southern shore. "I peered intently through my binoculars at the ships riding peacefully at anchor," Fuchida wrote later. "One by one I counted them. Yes, the battleships were there all right, eight of them! But the last lingering hope of finding any carriers was now gone. Not one was to be seen."

At 7:49, Fuchida ordered his rear radioman to send the command: "Attack!" Pearl Harbor's moment of doom was about to strike.

V

AIR RAID, PEARL HARBOR

Sunday morning, December 7, began at Pearl Harbor in typically peaceful fashion. Most of the U.S. Pacific Fleet was in port, and many of the officers and enlisted men had enjoyed Saturday night shore leave in nearby Honolulu. Now they were having breakfast on board their ships, or taking advantage of the exceptionally fine weather to lounge on deck. Here and there, sailors were polishing b.ass or wiping the dew off guns.

There was no anxiety whatever about a possible Japanese attack on Hawaii. True, on November 27, Admiral Stark in Washington, D.C., had sent a "war warning" to Admiral H.E. Kimmel, the new commander of the U.S. Pacific Fleet at Pearl Harbor. The message had said that "an aggressive move by Japan is expected within the next few days." But it indicated that the Japanese move would probably take place in the

Philippines, Malaya, or the East Indies. There was no mention at all of Pearl Harbor because, so far, the Japanese had managed to conceal that operation completely from our intelligence sources. Moreover, there was an assumption at Pearl Harbor that because of its great distance from Japan it was "immune" from attack. As a consequence, Admiral Stark's message did not ruffle the Pacific naval base, and no extraordinary precautions were taken to guard it against attack. The warning, however, had not gone completely unheeded. On November 28, Admiral Kimmel had dispatched the carrier *Enterprise* from Pearl Harbor to deliver Marine Corps fighter planes to Wake Island. On December 5, he had sent the carrier *Lexington* to deliver bombers to Midway. The third Pacific Fleet carrier, the *Saratoga*, had already left Pearl Harbor to be repaired on the U.S. West Coast. The result was that all three carriers were absent from Pearl Harbor on December 7. Their destruction would have been far more disastrous than the loss of our battleships, whose once-dominant role in naval warfare was already giving way to emphasis on aircraft carriers.

On December 6, Tokyo began transmitting a long dispatch to its embassy in Washington for delivery to the U.S. State Department the next day. It accused the U.S. government of ill-treating Japan, and concluded by breaking diplomatic relations with this country. This dispatch was intercepted and decoded by Army Intelligence and was in President Roosevelt's hands that evening. Roosevelt knew that it meant war, but nowhere did the message give any hint of an attack on Pearl Harbor, or anywhere else for that matter.

In accordance with Tokyo's instructions, on Sunday morning, December 7, the Japanese ambassadors requested an appointment with Secretary of State Cordell Hull at 1 P.M. to present their dispatch. Sunday was an unusual day for delivering diplomatic notes, and one o'clock was an unusual hour. Our Army and Navy intelligence units wondered whether the timing had any significance. One P.M. in Washington would be 7:30 A.M. at Pearl Harbor, but nighttime in the Philippines and Guam. So if the Japanese *were* planning to attack at that hour, Pearl Harbor would be the most likely place.

Admiral Stark was urged to notify Admiral Kimmel at once, but he hesitated. The overall defense of Hawaii was the responsibility of the U.S. Army, and Stark believed that General George C. Marshall, the Army Chief of Staff, should send the warning. Marshall, who had not yet seen the Japanese dispatch, was out that morning having his usual Sunday horseback ride. Marshall finally arrived at Stark's office at 11:15 and began reading the note. He agreed that it meant war, and that Pearl Harbor and Manila should be alerted at once. Marshall's warning was ready for radio transmission at noon, which was 6:30 A.M. Hawaiian time, more than an hour before the Japanese attack actually began. Unfortunately, the Army communications center was having problems of its own that day. It entrusted the message to a commercial telegraph agency, Western Union. The telegram was delivered to General Walter Short, the U.S. Army commander in Hawaii, by a boy on a bicycle hours after the attack was over.

The disaster might still have been averted, at least partially, if Army and Navy personnel at Pearl Harbor had been more alert. As December 7 began, five Japanese midget submarines were launched from larger submarines to sneak inside the port and launch torpedo attacks. At 3:40 A.M., a U.S. minesweeper sighted the periscope of one of these submarines less than two miles outside the harbor entrance. Word was passed by blinker signal to the destroyer *Ward*, which searched the area unavailingly for more than two hours. No one, however, thought it important enough to communicate this information to Navy headquarters. At 6:33, a Navy Catalina seaplane sighted a midget submarine (perhaps the same one), which was attacked and sunk by the *Ward* at 6:45. This time a coded message was sent by the *Ward* to Navy headquarters. Unfortunately, there was a delay in decoding the message, and another delay in relaying the contents by telephone to Admiral Kimmel. The Admiral was rushing to Navy headquarters in response just as the bombs began to fall.

Still another opportunity was lost when, at 7:02 A.M., two Army privates manning a radar unit on northern Oahu observed large blips on their screen. The blips indicated that a large formation of planes was approaching the island at a distance of 132 miles. The soldiers telephoned this information to an Army center, but the young officer who answered told them not to worry about it. He was expecting a flight of B-17 bombers from California that morning, and assumed that the blip was caused by these planes.

So it was that when Captain Fuchida gave the order to attack at 7:49, Pearl Harbor was taken completely by surprise. When the first bombs began to fall a few minutes later, it was believed that a very realistic air drill had been sprung on the Navy. Even when the Japanese red "meatball" insignia on the planes were spotted, it was assumed that the aircraft had been camouflaged for the sake of realism. It was 7:58 before Pearl Harbor understood what was really happening and broadcast this message: Air Raid, Pearl Harbor—THIS IS NO DRILL.

There were 94 ships in port, but the Japanese singled out as their main targets the eight battleships lined up alongside Ford Island within the harbor. The major attack was made by Kate bombers launching torpedoes at about 40-100 feet above the water. Almost at the same time, Val

30

dive bombers went to work on the battleships. In addition to conventional bombs, they dropped 16-inch armor-piercing shells that went through decks and exploded below. After dropping their bombs or torpedoes, most of these planes flew back over their targets, machine-gunning the stricken ships to kill as many sailors as possible.

One of the first battleships to be hit was the *West Virginia*. It took six or seven torpedoes on its port side, and two bombs as well. Yet the *West Virginia* fared better than some ships that suffered fewer hits. An alert officer saw the first Japanese bomb fall on Ford Island and promptly gave an order that brought everyone up to the deck on the double. This undoubtedly saved hundreds of men from being trapped below. Only the ship's antiaircraft guns on the starboard side were still functioning, and they opened fire within two minutes. Though the ship was listing badly to port side, quick counter-flooding allowed it to settle on the bottom without capsizing.

The heroic crew continually fought fires on the ship though frequently dive-bombed and strafed. The *West Virginia* lost 105 officers and men out of about 1500. These light casualties were due mainly to the quick alert and the excellent discipline that prevailed.

Other ships were not so fortunate. Within one minute of the attack, the *Arizona* was torn apart by torpedo and bomb explosions. One bomb penetrated to the ship's forward magazine, where munitions were stored. The ensuing blast wrecked half the ship and caused it to settle so fast that hundreds of sailors were trapped and drowned below. Even so, survivors opened fire on the enemy planes with machine guns, and the ship was not abandoned until 10:32. The *Arizona* lost 1,103 officers and men out of about 1400. These casualties accounted for more than half of those suffered by the entire fleet at Pearl Harbor.

Only one of the eight battleships attempted to escape the harbor and get out to sea. The *Nevada* was in the midst of its morning flag-raising ceremony and the ship's band was playing the national anthem when two Japanese planes came in to strafe it. The men continued to stand at attention until the band finished the anthem. Then they rushed into action with machine guns and antiaircraft batteries. One torpedo tore an enormous hole in the *Nevada*'s side, flooding many compartments but leaving the ship's power plant undamaged. Soon after, the ship came under heavy attack by dive bombers; two or three hits caused many casualties and heavy damage. At that point the *Nevada*'s senior officer made the decision to get up steam and move the ship out to sea. As the *Nevada* steamed down the main ship channel, it was pounced upon by another group of Val dive bombers. For a while, the smoke and spray from hits and near-misses almost concealed the battleship from view. Yet the crew never stopped firing its antiaircraft guns, and somehow the *Nevada* survived, though it didn't reach open sea. It was finally beached opposite the southern end of Ford Island rather than risking the chance of sinking in the main channel and blocking it. Yet the *Nevada*'s gallant attempt to exit the harbor did more to lift American morale at the scene than any other event that morning.

While "Battleship Row" was being devastated, other Japanese planes were concentrating on knocking out U.S. air power on Oahu. At the Naval Air Station on Ford Island, dive bombers destroyed or badly damaged 33 of the Navy's best aircraft within minutes. Vals and Zero fighters also made short work of the Catalinas at the Navy's nearby seaplane base. Three of the seaplanes were out on patrol at the time and were spared destruction. Of the rest, 27 were destroyed and six others damaged. At the Marine air field, Zeros swooped as low as 20 feet from the ground, attacking parked planes with short bursts of incendiary, explosive, and armor-piercing bullets. A second wave of Zeros and Vals continued the destruction until most of the 49 planes based there were shattered. At Wheeler Field, 62 of the Army's new P-40 fighters were parked in neat rows with wing tips touching. (This had been done to facilitate guarding them against possible sabotage.) Almost all of them were wiped out by a flight of nine Zeros shortly after nine o'clock. The same scenes of destruction took place at other fields on Oahu despite the brave efforts of pilots and ground crews to improvise hasty defenses.

By 10 o'clock, the Japanese attack on Hawaii was over, and the last of the enemy planes were returning to their carriers. Pearl Harbor lay hidden under a heavy blanket of smoke. The Japanese had accomplished their objective, which was to cripple the U.S. Pacific Fleet so it could not interfere with Japan's conquest of Southeast Asia in the months ahead. They had done their job well: All eight battleships, and six other warships, had either been destroyed or badly damaged. Half the aircraft on the island had been wiped out. In human terms, more than 2400 Americans had been killed and almost 1200 wounded. The cost of the attack to the Japanese had been 29 planes and 55 men.

Despite the devastation in Hawaii, there was a glimmer of hope for the United States as it suddenly found itself thrust into war with Japan and its allies, Germany and Italy. Our three Pacific aircraft carriers were safe, and they automatically became the principal weapon of the U.S. Fleet in the war against Japan. Our Navy soon learned to use these carriers with great skill, as the Japanese were to discover at the Battle of Midway.

For the Japanese, the attack on Pearl Harbor had proved more successful than anyone had expected. Yet the self-congratulations were tempered by the knowledge that they had failed to inflict any damage on our carriers. Even as the Pearl Harbor Striking Force was sailing back to Japan, some of its officers were already hatching plans for an all-out effort to destroy them.

VI

A HIT-AND-RUN STRATEGY

Within hours after the attack on Pearl Harbor, the Japanese launched other air strikes against Hong Kong, Singapore, Guam, Wake Island, and the Philippines. It was the beginning of a "blitz" (lightning) campaign to conquer all Southeast Asia. Against their ill-prepared American, British, and Dutch foes, the Japanese rolled southward with such rapidity that they exceeded even their own timetables. In four short months, Japan had won its Greater East Asia Co-prosperity Sphere, a vast area stretching south to Australia and west to India.

These were dark times for the United States and its allies, but in Japan they were the best of times. Stimulated by their unprecedented successes, Japan's militarists were eager for new conquests. As one Japanese naval commander commented, they had succumbed to "Victory Disease." They believed that further expansion should be pursued at once, instead of waiting for their newly-won empire to be consolidated.

The only question that divided Japan's military leaders was the direction of their next offensive move. There were plenty of ideas. One proposal, made by Rear Admiral Matome Ugaki of the Japanese Combined Fleet, was for a move east aimed at the invasion and capture of Hawaii. This was rejected when staff officers who studied the idea pronounced it too risky. Another proposal by the Combined Fleet was for a move west—the invasion and capture of the island of Ceylon in the Indian Ocean. This plan was vetoed by the Japanese Army, which was then entertaining ideas of joining Nazi Germany in its war against Soviet Russia. As a consequence, the Army did not want to commit large forces to Ceylon. A third proposal, made by the Naval General Staff, was for a move south—an invasion of Australia. This plan was also vetoed by the Army, and for the same reason.

Finally the staff of the Combined Fleet came up with yet another plan for taking the offensive. This plan was less ambitious than its original proposal to invade Hawaii, and would not require large Army forces to support it. It called for the capture of Midway Atoll, the tiny U.S. outpost about 1100 miles northwest of Hawaii. What was the object of seizing Midway? For some time, the Combined Fleet had been disturbed by a number of hit-and-run raids conducted by U.S. aircraft carriers against Japanese-held islands. Although these raids were mere flea bites in the overall picture, leaders of the Combined Fleet felt that Japan's empire could not be considered secure as long as U.S. carriers were prowling the Pacific. The capture of Midway, and its use as an advance base for Japanese air patrols, would act as a deterrent against these raids. At the same time, it was calculated that a Japanese move against Midway might bring out the U.S. Pacific Fleet in force. That would give the much larger and more powerful Japanese Fleet an opportunity to destroy its enemy in a decisive battle. Admiral Yamamoto strongly supported the Midway invasion proposal. "In the last analysis," he said, "the success or failure of our entire strategy in the Pacific will be determined by whether or not we succeed in destroying the U.S. fleet, *more particularly its carrier forces*."

All that was needed now to activate the Midway plan was the approval of the Naval General Staff. But the Naval General Staff was no more receptive to this plan than it had been to the proposal to attack Pearl Harbor. In the debate on Japan's next move, the Naval General Staff had supported an invasion of Australia to keep it from developing into a powerful U.S. base. When this scheme was vetoed by the Army, the General Staff had come up with a more modest alternative designed to isolate Australia and prevent U.S. supplies from reaching it. This would be accomplished by gradually extending Japanese control over the islands that lie north and east of the

Australian subcontinent. The first step in this operation had already been taken, and a second was scheduled for May. The Midway plan would interfere with the further development of the "isolate Australia" strategy.

Now the Naval General Staff and Admiral Yamamoto locked horns over which plan should have precedence. Spokesmen for the Naval General Staff found many flaws in the Midway proposal. Midway would be difficult to take, difficult to hold, and its strategic value in curbing U.S. carrier raids would be minimal. Furthermore, they strongly doubted that the U.S. Pacific Fleet would risk an encounter with the Japanese Navy for the sake of defending Midway.

Admiral Yamamoto replied that the best way to isolate Australia was to destroy the U.S. carriers. Without them, he said, America would be unable to maintain its supply line to Australia. "We believe," he added, "that by launching the proposed operation against Midway, we can succeed in drawing out the enemy's carrier strength and destroying it.... If, on the other hand, the enemy should avoid our challenge, we shall still realize an important gain by advancing our defensive perimeter to Midway...."

Once again the Naval General Staff had to knuckle under to Admiral Yamamoto, but by the middle of April, 1942, it was still quite skeptical about the Midway operation and continued to haggle over details. On April 18, however, an event took place in Japan that quickly put an end to further debate: Tokyo was bombed by U.S. war planes launched from an aircraft carrier.

The U.S. raid on Tokyo was almost as astonishing to the Japanese as their raid on Pearl Harbor had been to us. The actual damage inflicted on Tokyo was minor compared with later raids carried out in World War II, and only a fraction of what the Japanese had inflicted upon Hawaii. Most of the damage was psychological. Japan's armed forces, which were imbued with the idea that their foremost duty was to protect the Emperor from danger, were mortified. They were also considerably perplexed: They could not figure out how the Americans had executed the raid.

The Tokyo raid was conceived in January, 1942, as America's "answer to Pearl Harbor." Japan's capital was the logical target for retaliation. The question was, how could it be reached by our planes? Japanese patrol boats guarded the approaches to Tokyo from a distance of at least 500 miles eastward. Land-based aircraft patrolled the approaches from a distance of 300 miles. Carrier aircraft did not have the range to hurdle these barriers. If the carriers penetrated close to the Japanese homeland, they would be pounced upon by land-based aircraft and have little chance of survival. Finally it was suggested that the Army Air Force's B-25 medium bombers had the range to reach Tokyo if they could be launched from an aircraft carrier. But even if they could take off from a carrier deck, there was no way they could land on one after their mission. These planes required too much room to set down on a carrier. A solution was proposed: the B-25's would not return to the carriers but would fly on to China and land in areas still controlled by our Chinese allies.

The Army Air Force was enthusiastic about the plan, and soon volunteers were chosen to fly and operate the 16 B-25's that would take part in the raid. (Sixteen were all that would fit on the flight deck of a single carrier.) The 70 officers and 130 enlisted men were trained and led by Lt. Col. Jimmy Doolittle, a celebrated flier. At an airfield in Florida, they practiced taking off from a runway no longer than the flight deck of a carrier. Later the planes were flown to California and loaded on the deck of the carrier *Hornet* at San Francisco.

The *Hornet* sailed on April 2, 1942, escorted by two cruisers and four destroyers. So far, the *Hornet*'s mission was a well-guarded secret. Only six officers actually knew about it. But the next day, the mission was announced to all the participants. According to the *Hornet*'s official report, "Cheers from every section of the ship greeted the announcement and morale reached a new high...."

On the morning of April 13, the *Hornet* was joined by another carrier, the *Enterprise*, commanded by Admiral William F. Halsey. The *En-*

terprise would provide combat air patrol for both carriers the rest of the way, for the *Hornet*'s own planes had been stowed below deck to make room for the B-25's. It was calculated that the bombers would have to take off at a point about 500 miles from Japan in order to have enough fuel after the raid to reach friendly Chinese territory. Admiral Halsey, the overall commander of the carrier task force, planned to launch from that distance late on the afternoon of April 18. The raid would be a night attack, with 13 planes attacking Tokyo and three striking at other cities.

In the early hours of April 18, when the two carriers were more than 700 miles from Japan, radar indicated the presence of Japanese patrol boats. Although the carriers shifted their course, they were unable to escape detection at daybreak; Tokyo would be quickly warned by radio. With the element of surprise gone, and the task force still about 650 miles from its objective, Halsey had to make a difficult decision. He could not afford to endanger his carriers any longer. Either he had to launch the B-25's now and risk their running out of fuel before reaching friendly Chinese airfields, or give up the mission completely. With Doolittle's approval, Halsey elected to launch the B-25's as soon as the bombing plans could be modified for a daylight attack.

Rough seas and heavy winds prevailed that morning, but all of the bombers lifted safely off the *Hornet*'s flight deck. By noon they were over

Tokyo where, surprisingly, they encountered little opposition. Tokyo's air defense forces were caught unprepared despite the early warnings they had received from Japanese patrol boats. They did not know that long-range U.S. Army bombers would be used in the attack. Consequently they estimated that the U.S. carriers would need several more hours to approach Japan and would launch their attack the next morning. The noon raid came as a complete surprise, and the B-25's had little difficulty carrying out their low-level bombing attacks against assigned military targets.

Not one of the bombers was shot down over Japan. Most of them managed to crash-land in friendly Chinese territory. Two had to come down in Japanese-held areas of China, and eight crewmen were taken prisoner. Japan's authorities were baffled by a raid executed by Army Air Force bombers. Could they really have been launched from aircraft carriers? Their doubts were dispelled after the captured fliers were tortured at length. All eight prisoners were tried by a military court and sentenced to die. Five of the sentences were later commuted to life imprisonment, but three men were executed.

Because the physical damage incurred by the bombers was minor, the raid was pooh-poohed in Japan as a "do-little" or "do-nothing" affair (a play on the name of Lt. Col. Jimmy Doolittle). But the psychological effect of the raid on Japan's military leaders was very great. The attack had endangered the "divine" Emperor Hirohito, and this could not be allowed to happen again. From now on, there could be no more opposition to Admiral Yamamoto's plan to lure the U.S. carriers into action at Midway and destroy them with an overwhelming preponderance of Japanese naval strength.

VII

YAMAMOTO'S MASTER PLAN

Late in April, Admiral Yamamoto and his staff were putting the finishing touches on the Midway plan. They were aboard the brand-new superbattleship *Yamato*, which at 62,000 tons was the largest warship in the world. Admiral Yamamoto had every reason to feel confident about the impending showdown with the U.S. Pacific Fleet. His plan called for the employment of about 200 ships, including no less than 11 battleships, eight carriers, 22 cruisers, 65 destroyers, and 21 submarines. It was, in fact, the most powerful fleet ever assembled. To oppose this huge force, the U.S. Pacific Fleet had three carriers, eight cruisers, 15 destroyers, and 19 submarines. By all odds, Midway should have resulted in the decisive victory that Admiral Yamamoto fully expected. The fact that it ended disastrously for Japan was due in large measure to a basic flaw in Yamamoto's plan of operations. Instead of concentrating his forces at Midway, he devised an elaborate scheme of entrapment that dispersed his armada over large areas of the Pacific. His reasoning was as follows:

The invasion of Midway would come as a complete surprise to the Americans. Once the U.S. Pacific Fleet learned of it, it would steam out of Pearl Harbor in full force to strike at the invaders. As soon as the Pacific Fleet had taken the bait, all of his forces would converge on the Midway area and annihilate the enemy.

The plan had all the elements of surprise that Yamamoto liked so much. Unfortunately for him, the U.S. Pacific Fleet did not play the role that he had intended for it, so his master plan came to naught. Even so, it might have worked if other circumstances had not gone against him as well.

Basically, Yamamoto divided his forces into five major groups and assigned different missions to each:

1. The Advance Expeditionary Force, comprised of 16 submarines. Most of them would be deployed between Hawaii and Midway. Their job would be to spot the U.S. Pacific Fleet after it had steamed out of Pearl Harbor and report its movements to Admiral Yamamoto.

2. The Northern Area Force, centered on two light carriers, the *Ryujo* and the *Junyo*. This force would strike the first blow on June 3, attacking objectives in the Aleutian Islands. These largely uninhabited, fog-bound islands stretch westward from Alaska. The purpose of the attack there was chiefly to decoy units of the Pacific

Fleet up north and weaken U.S. strength at Midway.

3. The Carrier Striking Force, centered on the six aircraft carriers that had attacked Pearl Harbor. It was scheduled to bomb Midway on June 4 and soften it up for the invasion forces that were to follow.

4. The Midway Occupation Force, consisting of troop transports guarded by a large group of battleships, heavy cruisers, and other warships. It was scheduled to begin the actual invasion of Midway on June 5 after dark. About 5,000 ground troops would be employed in the assault.

5. The Main Body, centered on seven battleships, including Admiral Yamamoto's flagship, the *Yamato*. This force would lie in wait about 400 miles west of Midway. As soon as the U.S. Pacific Fleet entered the Midway area, the Main Body would close in for the kill.

Early in May, war games were held aboard the *Yamato* to test the Midway plan and other contemplated operations. The facility with which the Japanese Combined Fleet carried out all its missions in tabletop maneuvers amazed a few skeptical observers. For example, a test situation developed in which the Carrier Striking Force was bombed by enemy land-based aircraft while its own planes were off attacking Midway. By the rules of the games, an umpire rolled dice to determine how many bomb hits were scored on the Japanese carriers. The dice indicated nine hits, and accordingly the umpire listed two carriers as sunk. Admiral Ugaki, however, overruled the umpire. He reduced the number of bomb hits to three, and restored one of the ships to "action." In similar fashion, the Combined Fleet managed to win victory after victory.

Among the more skeptical observers, some raised questions about the soundness of the Midway plan. Of what use would the battleships stationed hundreds of miles to the west be in the event the carrier force quickly ran into trouble at Midway? What plans had the carrier force made in case it was suddenly attacked by enemy carriers while its own planes were striking at Midway Atoll? These questions could not be answered satisfactorily for the simple reason that Admiral Yamamoto had not considered these possibilities. Yamamoto was counting on complete surprise in the Midway operation. He did not expect any naval opposition to develop until at least three or four days after Midway had been invaded and captured. By that time, all his forces would have closed in to crush the U.S. Pacific Fleet.

Despite the reservations of some officers, the Japanese on the whole were guilty more of over-confidence than of self-doubts. This was especially true of Admiral Nagumo's Carrier Striking Force. As Captain Fuchida wrote later, "We were so sure of our own strength that we thought we could smash the enemy Fleet single-handed, even if the battleship groups did nothing to support us."

Such unbounded optimism was supported by the impressive record of the Nagumo force in all its operations to that time, including Pearl Harbor. It had sunk five battleships, an aircraft carrier, two cruisers, and seven destroyers. It had damaged several other large warships, destroyed 200,000 tons of smaller warships and merchant vessels, and hundreds of Allied airplanes. So far, not one ship of the Nagumo force had even been damaged by enemy action.

While the Combined Fleet was conducting its tabletop games aboard the *Yamato*, developments were taking place near northeast Australia that would considerably affect the Midway invasion plan. As part of their "isolate Australia" strategy, the Japanese had begun a two-pronged attack aimed at seizing Tulagi in the Solomon Islands and Port Moresby in southeastern New Guinea. To support this operation, the Combined Fleet had dispatched two big carriers that normally operated with the Nagumo striking force. These were the *Shokaku* and *Zuikaku*, which had taken part in the Pearl Harbor attack and were scheduled to participate in the Midway operation.

In an effort to stop the latest Japanese offensive, Admiral Chester W. Nimitz, the new Commander in Chief of the U.S. Pacific Fleet, ordered the carriers *Lexington* and *Yorktown* into the Coral Sea. For two days, the Japanese carrier task force and the U.S. carrier task force searched for each other without success. But on May 7, search planes of both forces located their enemies and a major battle ensued. The Battle of the Coral Sea was the first naval duel in which all losses were inflicted by air action and no ship on either side sighted a surface enemy. The struggle lasted two days and in the end the Japanese losses were lighter than ours. The U.S. lost the carrier *Lexington* and the destroyer *Sims*. The Japanese lost a small carrier, the *Shoho*.

Of greater significance, however, was the fate of the *Shokaku* and the *Zuikaku*. The *Shokaku* had suffered bomb hits and required extensive repairs. The *Zuikaku* had lost a large number of planes and pilots and needed replacements. As a result, both of these carriers had to be withdrawn from the Midway operation. Had these two carriers been able to participate in the Battle of Midway, they might have tipped the scales in favor of the Japanese.

Oddly, the loss of the *Shokaku* and the *Zuikaku* for the impending Midway invasion did not disturb the Japanese at all. They believed that they had sunk not only the *Lexington*, but the *Yorktown* as well. Actually, the *Yorktown* had suffered heavy damage, but it was quickly repaired in time for the Battle of Midway. In any event, the Nagumo force was confident that it could carry out its assignment at Midway with only four carriers. On the evening of May 25, just hours before the main units of the Japanese Fleet were scheduled to depart for Midway, Admiral Yamamoto hosted a party aboard the *Yamato*. Many toasts were drunk to past and future triumphs. Warmed by the *sake*, a gift of the Emperor, the assembled officers shouted *banzais*. There were dreams of glory for everyone that night.

VIII

THE U.S. FLEET AND MIDWAY PREPARE

The success of Admiral Yamamoto's Midway plan depended upon the element of surprise. Its ultimate failure, therefore, lay chiefly in the fact that even before the Japanese Fleet had left its home bases, Admiral Nimitz had become aware of the plan and was preparing to repel the forthcoming invasion. The Navy's Combat Intelligence Unit at Pearl Harbor had been diligently intercepting Japanese radio messages and analyzing them. Although Intelligence could only decipher a fraction of each message because of the frequency with which the Japanese changed their codes, it was able to put the bits and pieces together and develop a fairly accurate picture of Japanese plans.

In early May, Intelligence was getting indications from radio intercepts of a massive operation involving most of the Combined Fleet, but no clues that might spell out the target. Gradually the code letters "AF" began cropping up more and more as a possible destination. Commander Joseph J. Rochefort, the head of the Intelligence Unit, had a hunch that AF stood for Midway, but he needed proof. On May 10, Rochefort made a suggestion to a member of Admiral Nimitz's staff. Could Midway be instructed to send a fake radio message stating that its machinery for converting salt water to fresh water had broken down? Rochefort hoped that the Japanese would intercept the message and identify the source as AF. Admiral Nimitz thought the idea was worth trying, and soon Midway radioed the phoney report. Two days later, Intelligence intercepted a Japanese radio message stating that AF was low on fresh water. That was all the proof needed. On May 14, Admiral Nimitz declared a state of "Fleet Opposed Invasion." It meant that the Navy, rather than the Army, would have responsibility for repelling the Japanese. Nimitz immediately began assembling his forces for the defense of Midway.

At this time, Nimitz had only three carriers at his disposal. The *Lexington* had gone down at Coral Sea, and the *Saratoga* was at San Diego, California, training a new air group. That left only the *Yorktown*, which had been ripped by a bomb hit at Coral Sea, and the two carriers of Admiral Halsey's task force, the *Enterprise* and the *Hornet*. All three of these warships were then in the South Pacific, thousands of miles from

Pearl Harbor. Admiral Nimitz ordered them back on the double.

Meanwhile Nimitz began taking steps to strengthen Midway Atoll against the expected invasion. Early in May, anticipating the possibility of an attack there, he had flown up to Midway and made a personal inspection of its defenses. Then he asked the two officers in charge what they would need to defend the outpost against an invasion. After being tóld, Admiral Nimitz said, "If I get you all these things, can you hold Midway against a major amphibious assault?" The officers assured Nimitz that Midway would hold.

Midway soon began to receive heavy reinforcements. On May 25, a cruiser arrived with a new Marine Corps outfit, the 2nd Raider Battalion commanded by Major Evans F. Carlson. "Carlson's Raiders," as they came to be known later in the war, fairly bristled with cartridge belts, grenades, and knives. The next day, another ship arrived with 16 Marine Corps Douglas dive bombers, seven Wildcat fighter planes, and 22 pilots. Most of the pilots were fresh out of flight school. Antiaircraft guns and a few light tanks were also delivered. The planes were especially welcome, for even though they were carrier castoffs, they were still much superior to the ancient Vindicator dive bombers and Buffalo fighters that had comprised Midway's air force until then. There were other reinforcements: The Navy increased the number of Catalina seaplanes to more than 30, and the Army Air Force sent 18 big B-17 bombers (Flying Fortresses) and four B-26's to beef up Midway's air strength. By June 4, the day the Japanese struck at the outpost, Midway had 121 combat planes and more than 3,000 officers and enlisted men for its defense.

While the new equipment was made ready, Midway prepared in other ways for the expected invasion. Barbed wire was strung along the beaches, underwater obstacles and mines were strewn, bomb-proof dugouts built, and guns sited to resist a landing. Most importantly, to prevent "another Pearl Harbor," the Navy Catalinas began flying daily search patrols over a wide area 700 miles west of Midway.

Meanwhile, Pearl Harbor was anxiously awaiting the return of its carrier task forces. Admiral Halsey's Task Force 16, centered on the *Enterprise* and the *Hornet*, steamed into view on May 26 and soon tied up inside the port. The ships were in fine fettle, but Admiral Halsey was not. This tough, aggressive commander had been stricken with a severe skin ailment and required immediate hospitalization. Admiral Nimitz asked him to recommend a replacement for the impending battle. Halsey nominated Rear Admiral Raymond A. Spruance, who normally commanded the cruisers and destroyers attached to Task Force 16. Although Spruance had no carrier experience and was not himself an aviator, he proved to be an excellent choice. A quiet, methodical man gifted with cool judgment, he would be an invaluable asset in the rough days that lay ahead.

Task Force 17, centered on the carrier *Yorktown* and commanded by Rear Admiral Frank Jack Fletcher, appeared at Pearl Harbor the following day, May 27. The *Yorktown* limped up the channel and went into drydock for repairs that afternoon. The ship was examined by a team of experts who found that its damage was quite severe. A bomb had exploded four decks down, and everything for a distance of 100 feet around was blistered, ripped, and twisted. The experts told Admiral Nimitz that it would take several weeks to repair the *Yorktown*. Nimitz replied quite seriously, "We must have this ship back in three days."

Almost immediately, more than 1400 workmen swarmed aboard the *Yorktown* and began rushing to get the warship repaired on time. Machinists, welders, electricians, and others worked in shifts around the clock for the next two days. There was no time to draft plans or make blueprints. Replacement parts were hastily improvised, rushed on board, and installed in record time. At 11 o'clock on the morning of May 29, the drydock was flooded and the *Yorktown* was towed back into the harbor while hundreds of men continued to work on it. That afternoon the carrier fueled, took on replacement planes, and was ready to sail out the next morning. The repair job had been completed in even less time than Admiral Nimitz had allowed.

By May 25, Nimitz had not only a clear picture of Yamamoto's intentions, but also of the approximate size of his forces and even the date set for the Midway attack. If the enemy's forces heavily outnumbered his own, Nimitz had other advantages. The most important one, of course, was knowing so much of Yamamoto's plan. Nimitz would not waste any large forces to defend the Aleutians. Rather, he would concentrate his strength at Midway and have his carriers ready and waiting there when the Japanese arrived. Another important advantage to Nimitz was Midway Atoll itself. It could accommodate more airplanes than a carrier, and was unsinkable. In effect, it would function as a stationary carrier in the impending battle.

Admiral Nimitz's orders to his task force commanders, Fletcher and Spruance, were to "inflict maximum damage on the enemy by employing strong attrition tactics." That meant launching air strikes against enemy ships. At the same time, Nimitz told them that they must be guided by the principle of "calculated risk." That meant "the avoidance of exposure of your force to attack by superior enemy forces without any good prospect of inflicting... greater damage on the enemy."

Admiral Spruance's Task Force 16 departed Pearl Harbor on May 28. Admiral Fletcher's Task

Force 17 departed the morning of May 30. On June 2, the two forces met at a position dubbed "Point Luck" about 325 miles northeast of Midway. Here they lay back and awaited word from Midway's search planes of the enemy's approach. The situation was quite the reverse of what Admiral Yamamoto was anticipating. Instead of sailing into a Japanese trap, the U.S. carriers were now preparing to ambush the enemy. The element of surprise was with our forces, not those of Admiral Yamamoto.

IX

THE INVADERS ARE SIGHTED

The main units of Admiral Yamamoto's huge armada began leaving their home bases on May 26, poised and ready for their objectives. Admiral Nagumo's Carrier Striking Force moved out that evening, followed by Yamamoto's Main Body two days later. Other units departed from Saipan and Guam on May 27. Morale on all the ships was high as the crews anticipated the certain destruction of the U.S. Pacific Fleet. "Our hearts burn with the conviction of sure victory," a Japanese officer wrote in his diary. No doubt he reflected the optimism of the entire fleet.

Nowhere was morale higher, however, than on the four carriers of Nagumo's Striking Force. Their orders were to "execute an aerial attack on Midway... destroying all enemy air forces stationed there" on June 4 in preparation for the invasion forces that would land the next day. To the crack pilots of the Nagumo force, this looked like an easy assignment. They were proven veterans, Japanese naval aviation's very best fliers.

Their planes were modern and first-rate. Japan's Zero fighter had a cruising speed of 240 miles an hour and was superior to the U.S. Wildcat, its opposite number, in speed, maneuverability, and rate of climb. It was not, however, as strongly built as the Wildcat. Japan's Kate torpedo bomber, which carried a crew of two or three, had twice the range and considerably more speed than its U.S. counterpart, the Douglas Devastator. The Kate cruised at 166 miles an hour; the Devastator made 100 miles an hour. An obsolete plane, the Devastator became a death trap for many U.S. fliers in the Battle of Midway. Only the U.S. Navy's new Dauntless dive bomber outclassed its Japanese rival, the Val.

The weather was fine for the first few days after the Carrier Striking Force left Japan, and the pilots practiced their bombing and torpedo runs, eagerly watched by the men on deck. But on May 30, the weather began to turn foul. Soon both the Striking Force and Yamamoto's Main Body, a few hundred miles behind it, were buffeted by strong winds, rain, and heavy seas.

Not just the weather was ominous, however. On May 29, Intelligence officers on Yamamoto's flagship, the *Yamato*, began to notice a sharp increase in the number of U.S. radio messages out of Hawaii. A high percentage of these intercepts were "urgent." This suggested that the U.S. Pacific Fleet had already discovered, or at least strongly suspected, the Japanese advance toward Midway. Other disturbing information was soon brought to Admiral Yamamoto's attention. U.S. seaplanes were reported patrolling 700 miles west of Midway. U.S. submarines were patrolling on a line 600 miles west of the atoll. Then came some more bad news — a hitch in Admiral Yamamoto's operational plan. Two Japanese seaplanes had been scheduled to fly over Pearl Harbor on May 31 to report on whether the U.S. Pacific Fleet was still in port. Because of the long distances involved in the flight, these planes would have to refuel at sea from submarines. The submarines were to wait for them at a point known as French Frigate Shoals. Unfortunately for Yamamoto's plan, when the Japanese submarines arrived, they found two U.S. Navy vessels already anchored there. The flight over Pearl Harbor had to be called off, and the news was promptly communicated to Admiral Yamamoto.

Yamamoto was disappointed by the failure of this mission, but he was sure that he would get news of the U.S. Pacific Fleet's movements from another source. His Advance Expeditionary Force of submarines was scheduled to straddle a line between Hawaii and Midway on June 3. These submarines would certainly spot the Pacific Fleet on its way up to Midway from Pearl Harbor. Yamamoto had calculated that the Pacific Fleet would move out of Pearl Harbor on June 4, after it had learned of the attack on Midway. That would give his submarines ample time to provide information on the strength and movements of the enemy forces. What Yamamoto did not know was that the U.S. task forces had already left Pearl Harbor and would be at Midway even before his submarines took their positions.

If Admiral Yamamoto was in the dark about the Pacific Fleet's whereabouts, he had plenty of information indicating that the U.S. at least suspected the Japanese thrust toward Midway and was taking steps to guard against it. Admiral Nagumo, whose Carrier Striking Force was spearheading the Midway invasion, had practically no information at all. Yamamoto was still hoping for surprise, and feared that radio communication with Nagumo would reveal their presence to the Americans. He insisted on maintaining radio silence; no warning was sent to Admiral Nagumo about the brisk U.S. activity monitored by the *Yamato*. Perhaps Yamamoto assumed that Nagumo's flagship, the *Akagi*, was receiving the same information as he was. If so, he was wrong. The *Akagi*'s radio-receiving capacity was quite limited. (Carrier radio masts had to be kept small to prevent interference with the take-off and landing of planes.)

On June 2, the Nagumo Striking Force encountered heavy fog, and navigation became extremely hazardous. On the bridge of the *Akagi*, Admiral Nagumo and his staff strained to keep the ship on course and to maintain its position in the formation. The fog, which persisted all day, had one advantage for Nagumo. His force was now coming within range of U.S. search planes. For the time being, at least, his ships were well hidden from them.

The following day, Nagumo's Carrier Striking Force was approaching Midway from the northwest. The Occupation Force, commanded by Vice Admiral Nobutake Kondo, was approaching the atoll a few hundred miles to the south of the carriers, and somewhat to the rear. At nine o'clock that morning, a Navy Catalina seaplane piloted by Ensign Jack Reid was flying almost 700 miles out from Midway. It was time for Reid to turn back, but he decided to go on for a few more minutes. Studying the ocean with his binoculars, Reid suddenly spotted a number of tiny, dark objects all coming in his direction about 30 miles away. Reid handed the binoculars to his co-pilot and asked, "Do you see what I see?" The co-pilot's reply was, "You're damned right I do!" There was no doubt that they had spotted part of Yamamoto's armada.

Popping in and out of the clouds for cover, Reid began tracking the Japanese ships. As Reid was to discover eventually, it is very difficult for an airplane pilot to identify correctly ships that appear on the ocean as little more than dots. This was borne out many times during the Battle of Midway when pilots on both sides repeatedly erred in identifying enemy warships. To Reid, the ships that he saw looked like a much more formidable force than it really was. Actually, Reid had sighted the Transport Group of the Midway Occupation Force. It was made up of 12 troop transports and freighters and their escort of 15 warships, most of them destroyers. The largest warship in the formation was Rear Admiral Raizo Tanaka's flagship, the light cruiser *Jintsu*. Reid believed, however, that he had found the Japanese "Main Body," and at 9:25 radioed that information to Midway. Midway quickly asked him for more details. At 11 o'clock, Reid reported "eleven ships" steaming toward the atoll. Midway still had no idea whether this formation included any carriers, which were the No. 1 targets designated by Admiral Nimitz, but it could not afford to wait much longer to strike. "Hit before we are hit" was the guiding principle of the atoll's defenders.

Navy Commander C. T. Simard, the top officer at Midway, ordered nine Army Air Force B-17's to attack the invasion ships. This was the first attack any of the B-17 pilots had ever made. Led by Lt. Col. Walter C. Sweeney, whose bomber was nicknamed the *Knucklehead*, they flew toward the area where Reid (and later other search pilots) had last reported seeing the Japanese force. About 570 miles out, they spotted more than 20 ships and circled around them to attack from out of the sun. Then they made three high-level bomb runs, each plane dropping four 600-pound bombs.

The Transport Group was aware that it had been tailed that morning by U.S. search planes, but several hours had passed since then and nothing had happened. Suddenly a Japanese officer on the bridge of the *Jintsu* spotted the B-17's coming in and sounded the alarm. Antiaircraft fire opened up just before the bombs began to fall, but the attack was over within a few minutes. Later the inexperienced B-17 pilots reported what they believed to be true: two battleships or heavy cruisers and two transports had been hit and were sending up clouds of dark smoke. Actually, they had scored no hits at all, only one near-miss, and the heavy smoke they saw was pouring from the ships' stacks.

That evening, as the B-17's were landing at Midway, four Navy Catalinas were sent off to attack the same Japanese force. Night bombing at sea was quite unusual at the time, but these Catalinas were equipped with radar and it was hoped that they would be able to make contact. A few hours later, after a radar "fix," they spotted the Transport Group silhouetted by bright moonlight. Their low-level torpedo runs, made at 50-100 feet above the water, took the Japanese by surprise. One hit was scored on an oiler, and the explosion killed or wounded 23 men. The damage to the ship itself was negligible, and it managed to stay in formation.

The two ineffective attacks on the Transport Group by Midway-based planes were merely the opening shots of the forthcoming battle. "The whole course of the war in the Pacific may hinge on the developments of the next two or three days," a Navy Intelligence analyst at Pearl Harbor commented after receiving news of these developments.

Admiral Yamamoto had also been informed of the attacks on the Transport Group. He was surprised that these ships had been discovered even before Admiral Nagumo had launched his attack on Midway. He could have no illusions now that the Midway invasion was going to catch the Americans unawares. Yet even at this late hour, he was determined to maintain radio silence between himself and the Carrier Striking Force. Nothing, he felt, must give away the position of the carriers. Meanwhile, Yamamoto's Northern Force had already struck at the U.S. base at Dutch Harbor in the Aleutians. The carrier-launched raid, executed early in the morning of June 3, did considerable damage, but it completely failed in its main objective, which was to divert large U.S. forces from Midway.

A PHOTO HISTORY:

The Rising Sun in the
Pacific and the
Battle of Midway

Japanese Marines firing from behind sandbag barricade during attack on Chinese city of Shanghai, January, 1932.

U.S. gunboat *Panay* sinking in Yangtze River near Nanking, China, December 12, 1937, after Japanese attack.

Japanese capture of Nanking, December 14, 1937, was followed by devastation. Dead bodies filled streets.

U.S. battleship *Nevada* makes brave attempt to escape Pearl Harbor during Japanese air attack, December 7, 1941.

On Ford Island, stunned sailors watch smoke and flames from U.S. battleships. Navy planes in foreground were also hit.

Torn apart by explosions, battleship *Arizona* sinks with loss of more than 1100 of crew.

UPI

U.S. Army B-25 bomber takes off from the carrier *Hornet* to raid Tokyo, April 18, 1942.

U.S. carrier *Lexington* on fire and listing during Battle of Coral Sea, May 8, 1942.

UPI

Rear Admiral Raymond A. Spruance (right) is decorated by Admiral Chester W. Nimitz after U.S. victory at Midway.

Admiral Isoroku Yamamoto

Vice Admiral Chuichi Nagumo

Lt. Commander John Waldron, leader of *Hornet*'s Torpedo 8 squadron, exemplified fighting spirit of U.S. pilots.

Japanese Kate was armed with a torpedo to attack warships.

Japan's Val dive bomber was outclassed by U.S. Dauntless.

Zero fighter had edge over U.S. Wildcat in speed.

U.S. Devastator torpedo bombers took heavy losses at Midway.

Dauntless dive bombers sank four carriers in Japanese force.

Wildcat fighter was built more solidly than Japanese Zero.

Both *Kaga* (top) and *Akagi* (center) were first laid down as battle cruisers. They were later converted to carriers by construction of elevated flight decks.

The *Hiryu* was smaller but more modern Japanese carrier.

U.S. carrier *Yorktown* shown during test run in 1937.

U.S.S. *Enterprise* going through trial run in 1938.

U.S.S. *Hornet* was commissioned by Navy in 1941.

U.S. dive bombers attacking Japanese carrier at Midway.

Yorktown suffers direct hit by Japanese bomber.

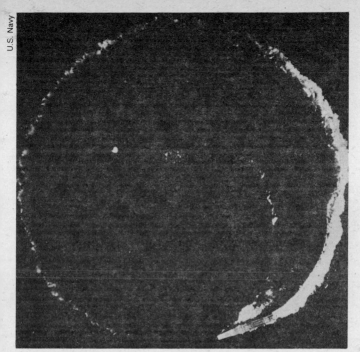

Soryu circles at high speed to avoid attack by U.S. dive bombers. Moments later, it received three lethal bomb hits.

Japanese cruiser *Mikuma* was wrecked by U.S. carrier planes in final action of battle.

X

THE JAPANESE STRIKE
AT MIDWAY

During the night of June 3-4, the opposing carrier forces were approaching each other on a potential collision course. By midnight, Admiral Nagumo's Striking Force was 340 miles northwest of Midway, and only about 100 miles from the point where it would launch its planes to attack the atoll. Nagumo's ships were steaming toward their objective at 25 knots. The U.S. carrier task forces, under the overall command of Admiral Fletcher, were about 300 miles northeast of Midway. Fletcher had received reports of the first contacts with the Japanese "Main Body," but doubted whether this was the enemy's carrier force which, he knew, would be approaching Midway from the northwest. On the evening of June 3, he set his ships on a southwest course. By dawn, this would bring him to a point about 200 miles directly north of Midway, a perfect position for launching a surprise attack on Nagumo's force — once it was sighted.

Nagumo's carriers reached their launching point about 4 A.M. June 4. In the predawn darkness, the first-wave attack planes were lined up and ready for the attack on Midway. Below decks, the pilots were treated to an extra-special breakfast topped off with cold *sake*. Captain Fuchida, who had led the air attack on Pearl Harbor, was aboard the flagship *Akagi*, but he would take no part in this action. He had been stricken with appendicitis the first night out from Japan, and was now recuperating in the ship's sick bay. His place was assigned to Lt. Joichi Tomonaga, a tough flight commander attached to the carrier *Hiryu*. Tomonaga was also a veteran of the Pearl Harbor strike.

Despite his weak condition, Fuchida managed to clamber up to the flight deck to watch the take-off. On the bridge of the *Akagi*, another invalid, Commander Minoru Genda, stood at Admiral Nagumo's side. Genda was the staff officer who had planned all of Nagumo's operations, including the Pearl Harbor attack. Now he was suffering from a heavy cold, but he too had left sick bay to observe the launching.

At 4:30, the order came from the bridge: "Commence launching!" The sea was calm and wind conditions were perfect. A Zero fighter revved up its engine, gathered speed along the flight deck, and rose into the air. The crew of the *Akagi* cheered and waved to the pilot. The others were launching at the same time. Within 15 minutes, the first wave of 108 planes was in the air. This formidable attack group consisted of 36 Kates, armed with bombs, from the *Hiryu* and the *Soryu*; 36 Val dive bombers from the *Akagi* and the *Kaga*; and 36 Zero fighters, nine from each carrier. After circling above the carriers briefly, the planes headed toward Midway, 240 miles to the southeast.

For a while, the flight decks of the carriers were silent. But then a new order blared out, "Prepare second-attack wave!" Immediately other planes were brought up on elevators to the flight decks and armed by the crews. The second wave of attack planes was prepared for a different assignment. It was to be held in readiness, as a reserve, in case the U.S. carrier task forces should suddenly turn up. Consequently, the second wave was armed for an attack on ships, rather than a land objective. This meant that the Kates were now fitted with torpedoes, rather than bombs. By five o'clock, when the sun was beginning to come up, these planes were lined up and ready to take off if needed. Nagumo had taken one other precaution against the possibility of U.S. carriers turning up unexpectedly. He had ordered seven search planes to scout the area to the east for 300 miles. These search planes were seaplanes that were catapulted from his cruisers. The last of them, the cruiser *Tone*'s No. 4 plane, was catapulted at 5 o'clock after a half-hour delay. Meanwhile, Nagumo kept one group of Zeros in the air to protect his ships from any intruders. Another was standing by on the deck of the *Akagi*.

So far, Nagumo's carrier force had not been sighted by U.S. search planes. It was still protected by a low cloud cover and poor visibility. But at 5:34, it was reported for the first time by a Catalina that radioed Midway, "Enemy carriers." At 5:45, the Catalina radioed another message: "Many enemy planes heading Midway, bearing 320 degrees, distance 150 miles." Both of these messages were picked up by Admirals Fletcher and Spruance, but their information about the Nagumo force was extremely sketchy. What was the position of the enemy carriers? What was their course and speed? How many were there? Then at 6:03 another radio message reached Admiral Fletcher. This one said, "Two carriers and battleships bearing 320 degrees, distance 180 miles, course 135 degrees, speed 25 knots." That position was about 200 miles southwest of the U.S. carrier task forces. Now, for the first time, Fletcher and Spruance knew the approximate location of the Japanese carriers, even though only two of them had been sighted. (The two battleships reported were part of the escort group.)Admiral Fletcher had launched a group of search planes earlier from the *Yorktown* and wished to recover them before proceeding to the attack. But at 6:07, he signaled Spruance to "proceed southwesterly and attack enemy carriers when definitely located. Will follow as soon as search planes recovered." Within minutes, Spruance's Task Force 16 was plunging toward Nagumo's position.

The air-raid alarm at Midway Island was sounded at 5:55, minutes after search radar had picked up the Japanese flight at a distance of 93 miles. Earlier radio messages reporting the enemy's presence had created confusion on the outpost, but now there was no doubt that "bogey aircraft" were fast approaching Midway. The first thing that had to be done was to get every plane possible into the air. None must be caught on the ground when the enemy arrived. A wild scramble to take the planes aloft ensued. The bombers and Catalinas, which would be useless for defense purposes, were ordered to disperse and stay clear of Midway. The job of stopping the attack was given to Major Floyd B. Parks' Marine Corps fighter squadron, which consisted of 20 antique Brewster Buffaloes and six obsolete Wildcats. Inside Midway's radar station, all eyes were fixed on the screen. It showed two blips, one the enemy, the other ours, sweeping toward each other.

The Japanese bombers were flying in V-formations at 12,000 feet with their fighter escorts directly above. The Marine fighters had climbed to 17,000 feet to intercept the attackers.

Captain John Carey spotted the Japanese formation first and radioed, "Hawks at angels 12 supported by fighters." ("Hawks at angels 12" meant enemy planes at 12,000 feet.) The Marine fighters dove at the Japanese group, setting their sights on individual targets. One Japanese plane caught fire and fell out of line, while another exploded in flames. Then, as the Marine fighters climbed for a second pass at the enemy, the Zeros tore into them. The Marine pilots tried desperately to shake the Zeros off, but their obsolete planes were easily outmaneuvered by the fast Japanese fighters. Cannon and machine-gun fire ripped into cockpits, tore wing flaps to shreds, and blew up gas tanks. Occasionally one of the Marine pilots would try a trick. With a Zero on his tail, he would cut the throttle, slowing his plane down to a crawl. Then he would watch the Japanese plane zoom by him. But within a short time, most of the Marine fighters had either been destroyed, or were out of action. One of the pilots shot down was Major Parks.

Now the Japanese attack force continued on to Midway virtually unmolested. Their strike would be carried out in three phases. First the Kates would bomb Midway at high altitude. Then the Val dive bombers would swoop down on chosen targets. Finally the Zeros would strike anything the bombers had missed.

At Midway, all antiaircraft guns were manned and ready, their crews scanning the sky toward the northwest. On the radar screen, it was clear that the Japanese planes were coming in very fast, though to the gun crews they still looked like distant specks on the horizon. At 6:29, the radar unit fixed their distance at eight miles. A minute later, the order was given to fire when they were within range. At 6:31, every antiaircraft gun on the atoll opened fire.

Two of the attackers burst into flames, yet one of them kept coming in. When it finally fell, the gunners cheered themselves hoarse. At 6:34, the Japanese formation was directly overhead, and sticks of bombs began falling everywhere. The first bombs made a shambles of the seaplane hangar, the mess hall, post exchange, and an antiaircraft gun shelter. Then the dive bombers struck, demolishing the powerhouse, oil tanks, and the Marines' command post. The hospital and storehouses were set on fire, and the gasoline supply system damaged. (All Midway planes had to be fueled by hand after that.) Finally the Zeros swept in, strafing every likely target remaining.

The atoll's defenders fought back with everything they had. Some of the men even grabbed small arms and fired at the Japanese with rifles and pistols. Meanwhile a few badly damaged Marine fighters straggled in, hotly pursued by Zeros. In some cases, the Marine pilots led the enemy planes right into antiaircraft fire, and more than one Zero was destroyed.

By 6:50, the attack was all over, and the

Japanese planes began returning to their carriers. The All Clear signal was sounded at 7:15, after which Midway's commanders took stock of their losses. Hardest hit was the Marine air group. When Lt. Col. Ira E. Kimes radioed his pilots to land and refuel, only six responded. In all, 17 Marine fighter planes and their pilots were lost, and seven other planes were severely damaged. Only two planes were still in condition to fly.

Despite the almost complete loss of the Marine fighter group and the heavy damage inflicted on the atoll's installations, Midway's defenders had a few things going for them. Because their shelters and dugouts were amply protected by sandbags, the men on the ground suffered few casualties — 11 dead and 18 wounded. Beyond that, most of Midway's planes were still intact. Only an old utility plane had been caught on the ground when the Japanese attack began. One other "aircraft" was lost, a decoy made of junk parts. It was called the "JFU," short for Jap Fouler-Upper, and it played its part well.

The Japanese were keenly disappointed at not finding large numbers of planes on the ground when they struck the island. The destruction of Midway's air strength had been the main objective of their mission. Obviously, the Americans had been alerted and had sent all their planes aloft. Lt. Tomonaga, the Japanese flight commander, decided it would be necessary to strike again at Midway after its planes returned to refuel. At 7 o'clock, Tomonaga radioed the *Akagi*, "There is need for a second attack." For Admiral Nagumo, this would be the beginning of an ever-increasing dilemma.

XI

MIDWAY COUNTERATTACKS

The call for a second strike against Midway had not been anticipated by Admiral Nagumo, and it required some discussion with his staff officers. Rear Admiral Ryunosuke Kusaka, Nagumo's chief of staff, was concerned about using the carriers' reserve planes for a second strike. What if enemy carriers should show up in the meantime? Commander Genda favored a second strike. He doubted whether any U.S. warships were in the vicinity. So far, the Japanese search planes had not sighted any, so why not finish off Midway as soon as possible?

Admiral Nagumo knew, of course, that the Americans had been receiving information about his carrier force since about 5:32. That was when the first of several Catalina search planes had sighted his ships, and was in turn sighted by the Japanese. Zeros were ordered to shoot down the intruders whenever they appeared, but the Catalina pilots were so skillful at dodging in and out of clouds that they had successfully eluded their pursuers. They were still shadowing the Japanese carriers, and Nagumo knew it. However, his own search planes had found no evidence of a U.S. fleet, so perhaps Genda was right about a second strike against Midway.

If Nagumo needed any further convincing, it came within a very few minutes. At 7:05, a formation of 10 U.S. bombers was sighted approaching the carrier force and air-raid alarms were sounded. This air group, which consisted of six Navy Avenger torpedo planes and four Army B-26's (Marauders), had taken off from Midway before the Japanese struck the atoll. Once the position of the Japanese carriers became known, these and other Midway bombers were ordered to attack them.

Almost as soon as the U.S. planes sighted Nagumo's ships, they were pounced upon by Zero fighters. Five of the Avengers were shot down, and none got close enough to launch its torpedoes effectively. The B-26's, which followed the Avengers in, fared only a little better. One of them fell quickly, but the three others kept boring in and finally released their torpedoes. The missiles headed straight for the *Akagi*, but fortunately for the carrier, they were very slow. The *Akagi* maneuvered and turned, dodging all the torpedoes. Everyone aboard breathed a sigh of relief.

After launching their torpedoes, the B-26's started to pull out of their runs, swinging sharply to the right and away. One of them, hit by anti-aircraft fire, never made it. It hurtled straight toward the *Akagi*'s bridge, its white stars plainly visible. Everyone on the bridge, including Admiral Kusaka, ducked. But the plane cleared it by inches and then plunged into the sea. Only one Avenger and two B-26's survived the attack.

Admiral Nagumo had no doubt that these planes had come from Midway. He knew what he had to do now. At 7:15, he ordered his second-wave planes, which presently were armed for an attack on ships, to be rearmed for a strike against Midway. This meant that the Kates on the *Akagi* and *Kaga* would have to be taken below and switched from torpedoes to bombs. (The order did not affect the *Hiryu* and the *Soryu*, whose Kates had gone out with the first-attack wave.) Rearming these planes was a back-breaking job, but the flight crews worked furiously to get it done quickly. The Japanese hoped to get these planes rearmed and into the air before Lt. Tomonaga returned with the first wave.

While this work was going on below the flight deck, Admiral Nagumo and his staff received a jolting radio message. At 7:28, the cruiser *Tone*'s No. 4 plane, which had been sent aloft that morning to search for enemy ships, reported: "Sight what appear to be 10 enemy surface ships in position bearing 10 degrees, distance 240 miles from Midway. Course 150 degrees, speed over 20 knots." Nagumo had not expected that enemy warships would turn up so soon. Not only were they close by, but apparently they were set to ambush him. Ironically, if the *Tone*'s No. 4 plane had not been a half-hour late in getting off that morning, Nagumo would not have been faced with his present dilemma. He would have been informed of these warships *before* he had decided on a second strike against Midway, and would not have ordered his planes rearmed.

Nagumo pondered his dilemma and then came to a decision. At 7:45 he ordered the rearming of the Kates to be suspended at once and signaled new orders to his entire force: "Prepare to carry out attacks on enemy fleet units."

Nagumo was concerned, however, about the makeup of the U.S. force sighted by the *Tone* search plane. The information that he had received—"10 enemy surface ships"—was not very specific. Were any of the ships carriers? If so, he must strike at them quickly, before they struck at him. If not, the situation was less urgent, and perhaps he even had time to carry out a second strike against Midway before disposing of the enemy ships. Now, to make sure, Nagumo radioed the pilot of the *Tone* search plane a brusque order: "Ascertain ship types and maintain contact."

Admiral Spruance's Task Force 16, consisting of two carriers, six cruisers, and nine destroyers, had been steaming southwest following Fletcher's orders to "attack enemy carriers when definitely located." All ships were now in a state of combat readiness. On the carriers, the pilots were restlessly waiting in their squadron ready rooms for the order to go up.

Spruance intended to launch his planes at nine o'clock, when his force would be less than 100 miles from Nagumo's carriers. At that distance, his planes would have enough fuel to reach the Japanese carriers, attack them, and then return. But as reports of the strike against Midway began coming in, Spruance's chief of staff, Captain Miles Browning, argued in favor of an immediate launching. It was essential, he said, to attack before the enemy became aware of their presence.

Now Admiral Spruance had a difficult decision to make. If he launched his planes at seven o'clock, as Browning urged, their distance from the enemy ships would be 155 miles. It meant that many of them would not have enough fuel to get back to their carriers and would have to splash down at sea. Then destroyers would have to rescue them, if possible. Spruance decided that the "calculated risk" was worth taking. Approximately 20 minutes before Nagumo ordered his second-wave planes to be rearmed, Spruance ordered his own planes to strike at the Japanese. At last his fliers in the ready rooms heard the order they had been waiting for: "Pilots, man your planes!"

Spruance made another important decision at

this time. This was going to be an all-out attack. Except for some fighters needed to patrol over his task force, every available plane would be flung at the Japanese. Nothing would be held back as a reserve. In all, 67 Dauntless dive bombers, 29 Devastator torpedo bombers, and 20 Wildcat fighters would be sent up.

The launching began at 7:02. Within a half hour, when it was far from completed, Spruance learned that his task force had been sighted by a Japanese search plane. (It was the *Tone*'s No. 4 plane.) Spruance feared that he had now lost the advantage of surprise. But even if the Japanese had learned of his presence, their carriers would still have to proceed on a course toward Midway to retrieve their first-wave planes. So there was no thought of calling off the attack. Instead, it was essential to speed it up. Those squadrons already in the air would have to proceed on their mission at once without waiting for the others to be launched. Because of the urgency of the situation, it would be impossible to deliver a coordinated attack.

While Admiral Nagumo impatiently awaited further information from the *Tone* search plane, his carriers were moving closer to the point where they were scheduled to recover the first-wave planes. The four carriers were steaming in a boxlike formation surrounded by a protecting screen of two battleships, three cruisers, and 11 destroyers. The *Akagi* and the *Kaga* formed the two starboard (right side) corners of the box. The *Hiryu* and the *Soryu* formed the two port (left side) corners.

It was extremely difficult for the carriers to maintain their neat formation, however, for they were encountering persistent attacks from Midway-based planes. At 7:55, 16 Dauntless dive bombers led by Marine Corps Major Lofton Henderson came in to attack the Striking Force. Because of the inexperience of most of the pilots, Henderson had decided not to dive-bomb but to make long, shallow dives instead. (This was called glide-bombing. It required less skill than dive-bombing, but certainly no less courage.) Although the *Hiryu* had some anxious moments as bombs dropped by one Marine plane bracketed it, no hits were scored and the attack was beaten off with heavy losses. Only eight of the dive bombers survived the onslaught of Zero fighters, and six of them were damaged beyond repair. Major Henderson was one of the casualties.

The Japanese were puzzled by what they considered the amateurish, though brave, tactics of the American fliers generally. The Japanese pilots were, of course, professionals, whereas a year or two before most of the U.S. pilots had been accountants, clerks, salesmen, and truck drivers who had never even flown a plane.

The next attack on the Nagumo force was delivered by a flight of 15 Army Air Force B-17's (Flying Fortresses). Led by Lt. Col. Sweeney, they approached at 20,000 feet, an altitude from which the Japanese ships looked like bathtub toys. Yet they could see the enemy ships twisting and turning in evasion maneuvers, and soon understood the reason. The Japanese were being attacked by Major Henderson's bombers far below. Soon afterward, the Army fliers released their heavy bomb loads, but scored no more than a few near-misses. The Zeros respected these big bombers that bristled with machine-gun turrets, and did not attack them aggressively. All of the B-17's returned with little damage.

The final attack by Midway-based planes came immediately after the B-17's had pulled away, at 8:20. It was carried out by 11 Marine Corps Vindicators, those ancient dive bombers that were nicknamed "Vibrators" and "Wind Indicators" by their pilots. Zeros swarmed all over them, and they had no chance of reaching the carriers. Instead, they shifted their attack to the nearest target, a battleship. All their bombs missed. The Marine pilots headed for home almost skimming the water for protection. Nine managed to return safely.

The Striking Force had undergone every conceivable kind of attack by land-based planes — level-bombing, dive-bombing, glide-bombing, and torpedo-bombing—and so far was unscathed. All its ships were intact, and heavy losses had been inflicted on the Midway planes. There was little time for self-congratulation, however. Lt. Tomonaga's first-wave planes were already beginning to return, and would have to be recovered soon.

Meanwhile, the *Tone*'s search plane had been sending Admiral Nagumo reports on the enemy surface ships it had sighted. Unfortunately for Nagumo, these reports were either vague or inaccurate. The first merely noted that the U.S. ships had changed their course slightly. Exasperated, Nagumo radioed the pilot, "Advise ship types." Minutes later, at 8:09, the *Tone* pilot reported, "Enemy is composed of five cruisers and five destroyers." This message, indicating that there were no carriers among the U.S. warships, was greeted with relief on the bridge of the *Akagi*. Admiral Kusaka's reaction was that a second strike against Midway could still be launched, and the enemy ships taken care of later.

Such optimism did not last long. At 8:20, the *Tone* search plane sent another message: "The enemy is accompanied by what appears to be an aircraft carrier bringing up the rear."

This report really shook up Admiral Nagumo and his staff. So an enemy carrier was present after all! Still, there was some doubt. The search plane pilot had qualified his identification with the words "appears to be." Soon after, the *Tone* pilot reported sighting two more enemy warships, "apparently cruisers." The size of the enemy force, more than anything else, convinced Admiral Nagumo that it must include at least one carrier. There were no more thoughts about a second strike against Midway now. The enemy carrier would have to be attacked first. The only question was, when? This would be the most fateful decision for Nagumo in the Battle of Midway.

XII

ZEROS VS. U.S.
TORPEDO BOMBERS

Having made his decision to strike at the U.S.
carrier task force, Admiral Nagumo was confronted with a number of serious problems. The
only planes that were then properly armed and
ready to launch for an attack on a carrier were the
36 Val dive bombers on the *Hiryu* and the *Soryu*.
Most of the Kates on the *Akagi* and the *Kaga* had
been switched from torpedoes to bombs before
Nagumo gave his order to suspend rearming
them. Though bombs launched at high altitude
could inflict severe damage, of course, generally
they were less effective than low-level torpedo
attacks upon a warship.

Even if Nagumo decided on an immediate
strike with the bombers available to him, regardless of how they were armed, there was still
another obstacle. Because of the attacks by
Midway-based planes, Nagumo had been forced
to send aloft practically all his Zeros to protect the
carrier force. They were now low on fuel, and

could not possibly escort the bombers on an attack mission. Nagumo had seen how easily the unescorted bombers from Midway had been shot down by his own fighters. The Kates and Vals would suffer the same fate, he was sure.

There was still another problem. Lt. Tomonaga's first-wave planes were now circling overhead. Many of them were in distress or running low on fuel. Unless they were recovered without delay, they would splash into the sea and more planes and pilots would be lost.

So Nagumo's dilemma was this: If he launched his bombers for an immediate attack, they would have to fly without fighter escort, and the Kates would not be properly armed. If he did not launch them immediately, he would have to clear the carrier flight decks in order to recover his first-wave planes. That would mean a considerable delay before he could get his attack on the U.S. carrier task force started. What to do?

Rear Admiral Tamon Yamaguchi, the aggressive commander of the *Hiryu* and the *Soryu*, could not understand why Nagumo had not yet ordered an attack on the enemy force. If Yamaguchi had had his way, he would have struck immediately with every plane available. At 8:30, Yamaguchi signaled an impatient message to his superior officer, Admiral Nagumo: "Consider it advisable to launch attack force immediately."

Admiral Kusaka, Nagumo's chief of staff, was

opposed to Yamaguchi's recommendation. It would be wiser, he said, to delay a while and do the job properly. First, he advised, recover both the Midway strike planes and the Zeros that had been sent aloft to fly combat patrol. While they were being recovered and refueled, the second-wave Kates would be sent below and switched back to torpedoes. Then, when all preparations were completed, a coordinated, all-out attack on the enemy carrier force would be delivered. Commander Genda also believed that the Midway strike planes should be recovered first. As a result, Nagumo rejected Yamaguchi's recommendation.

At 8:37, the first-wave planes were signaled to start coming in. The second-wave planes were sent below, the Kates among them to be rearmed. Once again the weary crews had to work frantically to get the planes ready. There was no time now for the normal precautions. The bombs removed from the Kates were not sent below to be stored in the magazine. Rather, they were hastily piled up on the hangar deck where they were extremely vulnerable.

By 8:55, Admiral Nagumo felt that he had the situation under control again. His ships were once more steaming in formation, his planes were rapidly being recovered, refueled, and rearmed. Ten minutes later, Nagumo signaled a confident message to his entire force: "After completing homing operations, proceed northward. We plan

to contact and destroy the enemy task force."
Nagumo also sent a radio message to Admiral
Yamamoto informing him of his intention.
Nagumo was not too concerned about reports
coming in from his search planes warning of the
approach of enemy carrier aircraft. He believed
that by turning his force northward, he would
throw the U.S. planes off his course and successfully elude them. At 9:17, the entire Striking
Force executed a turn and began heading north.
All Nagumo needed now was about one hour more
and he would be ready to deliver an all-out attack
on the American carriers. He had set the launching for 10:30.

Meanwhile, Admiral Fletcher's Task Force 17
had been following the same course and speed as
Admiral Spruance. Fletcher delayed launching,
however, until he felt sure there were no other
Japanese carriers around than those already reported. Having received no additional sighting
reports, he decided to launch at 8:38. In less than
a half hour, the *Yorktown* put 17 Dauntless dive
bombers, 14 Devastator torpedo bombers, and
six Wildcat fighters into the air. Admiral
Fletcher held another group of planes in readiness in case they were needed.

Nagumo's assumption that by turning north he
would elude the U.S. carrier planes proved to be
unrealistic. Only one group actually missed him
completely. This was a flight of 35 Dauntless dive
bombers and a fighter escort led by Commander

Stanhope C. Ring of the *Hornet*. When Ring did not find the Striking Force at its anticipated position, he headed south, pursuing Nagumo's former course. This turned out to be a wild-goose chase. Eventually, some of the dive bombers headed back to the *Hornet* while others landed at Midway to refuel. Two splashed into the lagoon. The fighter escort also tried to return to the *Hornet*. One by one the Wildcats ran out of fuel and had to ditch in the ocean.

The first U.S. carrier squadron to make contact with the Striking Force was Lt. Commander John C. Waldron's Torpedo 8 from the *Hornet*. Waldron's reputation was that of a hard taskmaster with a consuming desire to get at the enemy. Yet Waldron was fully aware that his slow Devastator torpedo bombers had little chance of surviving the battle. Even if they were not shot down in combat, they would not have enough fuel to return to the *Hornet*. Just before launching, Waldron had reported to Captain Marc Mitscher for instructions. According to Mitscher, Waldron "promised he would press through against all obstacles, well knowing his squadron was doomed...."

Waldron's 15 torpedo bombers were supposed to be joined by Commander Ring's flight, but the two groups were hidden from each other by layers of clouds and failed to link up. Continuing on its own, Torpedo 8 also missed the Japanese carriers at their estimated position. Waldron, however, sighted black smoke to the north and turned his group in that direction. At about 9:20, he sighted the enemy ships and led his squadron in toward Nagumo's outer screen of cruisers and destroyers.

The position of Nagumo's carriers was now an extremely vulnerable one. The flight decks were crowded with planes that were still being refueled and rearmed as fast as the crews could work. Bomb hits at this time could start incendiary chain reactions with devastating consequences. The moment Waldron's squadron was sighted on the horizon, Nagumo ordered, "Speed preparations for immediate launching!"

Waldron's squadron was still nine miles from the carriers when Zeros jumped it from above. One torpedo bomber went down immediately, but the rest of the squadron kept boring in. The Zeros attacked again and again, undeterred by the bombers' rear machine guns. One bomber after another fell, but Waldron kept on. His urgent radio messages to Commander Ring for help were futile; Ring's planes were nowhere near the action. Then Waldron's plane was hit, and soon the remaining torpedo bombers were shot out of the air by intensive antiaircraft fire. Torpedo 8 was wiped out without scoring a single hit on the Japanese force. Of the 30 men in the gallant squadron, just one, Ensign George H. Gay, survived. Gay was only slightly wounded and managed to get out of his plane before it sank. Gay inflated his Mae West life preserver jacket and hid under a rubber seat cushion from his plane. He was rescued by a Navy Catalina the following day.

The destruction of Torpedo 8 was complete by 9:36, when the *Akagi* ordered cease-fire. The Zeros that had run out of ammunition returned to their carriers to be rearmed. As soon as they were ready again, they went right back into the air, where they were sorely needed. Only a few minutes after the cease-fire, another flight of 14 U.S. torpedo bombers was sighted coming in. This one was Torpedo 6, launched from the *Enterprise*, and led by Lt. Commander Eugene E. Lindsey. Torpedo 6 was supposed to have a fighter escort, but there had been a foul-up and now the squadron was on its own. Torpedo 6 fared only a little better than Waldron's squadron. Ten of the 14 planes, including Lindsey's, were shot down. The few that were able to launch torpedoes scored no hits.

This attack had hardly been repulsed when, at 10 o'clock, yet another torpedo squadron came in to attack. Torpedo 3, launched from the *Yorktown*, had a fighter escort of six Wildcats. But the Wildcats were quickly jumped by a swarm of Zeros and had all they could do to defend themselves. Torpedo 3, led by Lt. Commander Lance E. Massey, had to make its run at the carriers alone. The squadron bore in courageously, as the others had, and another slaughter ensued. Twelve of the 14 planes were shot down, and again no hits were scored on the Japanese ships.

Perhaps at this moment Admiral Nagumo was beginning to feel less apprehensive about his carriers. Three separate attacks by U.S. torpedo bombers had been beaten back, and so far not one of his ships had even been scratched. Of course, his once-neat formation was now thoroughly jumbled, the result of frantic maneuvering to avoid torpedoes. But that was the least of Nagumo's worries. At 10:20, even before the last attack was completely repulsed, Nagumo ordered his own attack planes to launch when ready. He was a little ahead of his schedule, but he wasn't going to waste another minute to strike at the U.S. carriers. What Nagumo did not know was that it was already too late. The tide of battle was suddenly about to shift against him. Within a few minutes, all his plans would be doomed.

XIII

"ENEMY DIVE BOMBERS!"

Lt. Commander C. Wade McCluskey's two squadrons of Dauntless dive bombers had been the first to launch from the *Enterprise* that morning. They had circled above the carrier, waiting for the torpedo planes and their intended fighter escorts to launch also. Then, according to the plan, they would all attack the Japanese carriers together. But soon after, Admiral Spruance learned that his force had been discovered by the Japanese and ordered McCluskey to proceed on his mission without waiting for the other planes. In theory, McCluskey's 37 dive bombers should have reached the Japanese force before his torpedo group (Torpedo 6, commanded by Lindsey), but in fact he arrived minutes later. The reason was that McCluskey had had a difficult time locating the Japanese force.

When McCluskey reached the point where he expected to find the Japanese carriers, Nagumo's ships had already turned north. The flight leader saw only an empty sea beneath him. Like Commander Ring, McCluskey also searched to the south at first. Finding nothing, he decided at 9:35 to shift to the north. Twenty minutes later, he sighted a Japanese destroyer steaming at full speed on a northeast course. This was the *Arashi*, one of Nagumo's escort ships, which had fallen back to drop depth charges on a troublesome U.S. submarine, the *Nautilus*. (The *Nautilus* had been stalking the Japanese force since it was first located.) McCluskey assumed that the destroyer was racing to rejoin Nagumo's carriers, and promptly adopted its course. At 10:05, when some of his planes were already running out of fuel, McCluskey sighted the Japanese ships about 35 miles ahead. Soon he could see them quite clearly through his binoculars. All four carriers were rapidly maneuvering at this time to evade the attack by Lt. Commander Massey's Torpedo 3 squadron.

What surprised McCluskey the most was that the Zeros had not yet discovered his dive bombers and pounced on them. He did not know, of course, that the Zeros were so busy fighting off the torpedo bombers at low altitude that they did not see his high-flying dive bombers. Apparently the antiaircraft gunners had not observed them either, for the sky was clear of flak. So McCluskey's group was coming in unnoticed, and the target was wide open beneath it. The great courage of the torpedo bomber pilots had not been in vain. By pulling the Zeros down near the water, they had made it possible for the dive bombers to attack virtually unopposed.

How did the pilots of McCluskey's group feel at this moment? Lt. Clarence Dickinson said, "I had an intoxicating view of the whole Japanese fleet. This was the culmination of our hopes and dreams. Among those ships I could see two long, narrow, yellow rectangles, the flight decks of the carriers. That yellow stood out on the dark blue sea like nothing you have ever seen. Then farther off I saw a third carrier.... Suddenly, a fourth carrier!

"I could not understand how we had come this far without having fighters swarming over and around us like hornets. But we hadn't seen a single fighter in the air, and not a shot had been fired at us."

It was now 10:22. McCluskey ordered one squadron of dive bombers under Lt. Wilmer E. Gallaher to follow him down and attack the *Kaga*. He ordered another squadron under Lt. Richard H. Best to attack the *Akagi*. These carriers were fairly close to each other, whereas the *Soryu* was considerably to their starboard (right) and the *Hiryu* was now far off on the horizon. Both squadrons dove at 70 degree angles and at speeds of about 280 miles an hour.

On the *Kaga*, pilots waiting to man their planes for the coming strike were scanning the sky. Suddenly they saw a string of tiny black dots hurtling down on them. "Enemy dive bombers!" they shouted to the bridge, but their warning was too late. There was no time for the Zeros to climb up to intercept the bombers, and even the anti-aircraft gunners were too surprised to fire effectively.

At 1800 feet, McCluskey released his bombs and pulled out as fast as he could. The rest of the pilots in the two squadrons did the same, one after the other. One bomb just missed the *Akagi*, but a second hit near the aircraft elevator amidship and exploded on the hangar deck below. Instantly, the bombs that had been carelessly left there blew up, as did planes and gasoline tanks. Fierce fires engulfed the entire area and soon flames were shooting up the elevator shaft, through passageways, and toward the bridge. A third bomb hit the flight deck amid 40 Kates that were then being fueled and serviced. The planes blew up with a roar, and a terrific fire spread out of control. "It was just like hell," Admiral Kusaka said later. Then torpedoes began exploding, making it impossible for the fire-fighting crews to get at the flames.

Captain Fuchida described the scene on the *Akagi*: "Looking around, I was horrified at the destruction that had been wrought in a matter of seconds. There was a huge hole in the flight deck just behind the amidship elevator. The elevator itself, twisted like molten glass, was drooping into the hangar. Deck plates reeled upward in grotesque configurations. Planes stood tail up, belching livid flame and jet-black smoke. Tears streamed down my cheeks as I watched the fires spread, and I was terrified at the prospect of induced explosions that would surely doom the ship."

On the bridge, the *Akagi*'s navigator, Commander Gishiro Miura, found it impossible to steer the carrier. Its rudder was jammed, and the *Akagi* just kept going around in circles. Miura rang the telegraph indicator to "Stop," but the engine room failed to shut off the power. All other communications had been knocked out, so Miura sent a sailor below to investigate. Battling his way through flames, the sailor finally reached the engine room. The machinery was still running, but every man inside was dead, suffocated by the intense heat and fumes.

When the power was at last shut off, a new complication arose: the pumps stopped working and the hoses used by the fire-fighters went limp. Several hand pumps were rushed into use, but the flames kept gaining. Constant explosions killed or injured many of the fire crews.

Within minutes after the bombs struck, it was clear to Admiral Kusaka that the *Akagi* was doomed. It was already incapable of functioning as a flagship. Kusaka and others implored Admiral Nagumo to leave the carrier at once and transfer his command to another ship. But Nagumo was strongly devoted to his flagship and insisted upon remaining. Only when Kusaka reminded him of his duty to carry on as commander of the Striking Force did he reluctantly consent to leave. By this time, about 10:45, smoke and flames were blocking all the passages from the bridge. The only way out was to lower a rope from a window to the flight deck and clamber down. In this undignified fashion, Nagumo and his staff finally reached the flight deck. The deck was ablaze, bodies were strewn all over, ammunition was exploding, and guns were firing automatically. The officers dashed to the ship's side where a launch was waiting for them. They were soon transferred to the light cruiser *Nagara*, which became Nagumo's command ship for the remainder of the battle.

Crewmen continued to fight the fires aboard the *Akagi* all day, but by evening it was apparent that they could not be brought under control. Captain Taijiro Aoki then ordered all hands to abandon ship. While the injured were lowered into boats, others jumped over the side and were picked up by destroyers. A message was sent to Admiral Nagumo asking for permission to scuttle the stricken ship. Nagumo didn't answer, but Admiral Yamamoto, who had monitored the message, did. He turned down the request. Yamamoto was also strongly devoted to the *Akagi*, and hoped to save it.

The burning hulk drifted throughout the night. At 4:50 A.M., June 5, Yamamoto accepted the inevitable and gave the order to scuttle the

Akagi. Just before sunrise, it was sunk by a torpedo from a Japanese destroyer.

The *Kaga*, which was struck at the same time as the *Akagi*, fared no better. The first three bombs that hurtled down toward it were near-misses. They created harmless geysers of water as they exploded. But in the next moment, four bombs scored direct hits on the flight deck. One of them landed just forward of the bridge and struck a small gasoline truck that was standing there to service planes. The truck exploded in flames, killing everyone on the bridge, including Captain Jisaku Okada. The other bombs set fire to planes that were being refueled, penetrated the hangar, and set off explosions in a magazine. Furious fires broke out almost everywhere. The desperate efforts of the crew to contain them were pitifully ineffective. Soon there was hardly any place on the ship that was not in flames.

Some of the crew found refuge on the starboard boat deck, while others huddled on a narrow ledge along the side of the ship about 20 feet above the water. When all hope of containing the fires was lost, men began jumping into the sea to save themselves. One of those who jumped was Commander Takahisa Amagai, who had become the *Kaga*'s senior officer after the holocaust on the bridge. No formal order to abandon ship was ever given.

Just before 2 P.M., when the burning carrier was "dead" in the water and beginning to list, a new danger confronted the survivors. A torpedo was seen streaking toward the *Kaga* at a distance of 1,000 yards. In all probability, it was fired by the U.S. submarine *Nautilus*, which was still dogging the Japanese force. The men who were huddled on the ledge above the water jumped in and swam frantically to get away from the ship. The torpedo missed, and so did another fired moments later. A third torpedo struck the carrier, but it proved to be a dud. The missile broke in two and one part remained afloat. Ironically, some of the *Kaga*'s sailors used it as a raft until they were rescued by Japanese destroyers.

Early in the evening, after all survivors had been picked up, the burning *Kaga* was rocked by internal explosions. At 7:25, it slipped into the sea, its red-hot metal hissing as it went down.

At almost the same moment that McCluskey's squadrons were attacking the *Akagi* and the *Kaga*, another squadron of dive bombers was striking at the *Soryu*. This group, led by Lt. Commander Maxwell F. Leslie, had been launched from the *Yorktown*. Although it had started out more than an hour after McCluskey's bombers left the *Enterprise*, it had caught up to them by flying an almost direct course toward the enemy fleet. Selecting the *Soryu* as his target, Leslie dove from 14,500 feet, followed by the other 16 bombers of his group in three waves.

To Lt. Paul A. Holmberg, the big red circle painted on the flight deck looked like a good target and he set his sights on it. He could see lights flickering from the ship, and soon flak was exploding near his plane. The *Soryu* gunners, at least, had not been taken by surprise. At 2500 feet, Holmberg pressed his bomb-release button and pulled out of his dive. A moment later, a huge column of smoke was billowing up from the *Soryu*. Three lethal hits were scored on the carrier in as many minutes, and the entire ship burst into flames. When fire penetrated the torpedo storage room, the subsequent blast virtually demolished the *Soryu*. At 10:45, only 20 minutes after the carrier was struck, Captain Ryusaku Yanagimoto had to order all hands to abandon ship. Some men struggled to lower boats into the water, but most jumped over the side to escape being trapped by the flames. Captain Yanagimoto, however, refused to leave his ship. From the bridge, he shouted "Long live the Emperor!" to the men in the water.

The *Soryu* burned all day as destroyers were picking up the survivors. Toward evening, the fires subsided, and a Navy wrestling champion was sent aboard to remove Captain Yanagimoto by force, if necessary. When Yanagimoto refused to budge, the sailor lost his nerve. He left the ship in tears. The *Soryu* went down with its captain aboard at 7:13.

The dive bombers that had attacked the three carriers that morning ran into trouble almost as soon as they leveled out. By that time, they were in range of the Zeros, which had been climbing to intercept them. Now the Zeros were out to gain revenge, and many of the dive bombers were attacked relentlessly. McCluskey was pursued by two Zeros for about 35 miles. Each time the fighter planes dove on him, McCluskey dodged and weaved, while his rear gunner, W.G. Chochalousek, tried picking off the attackers with his twin-barrel machine gun. A burst fired by one of the Zeros shattered the cockpit and McCluskey's left shoulder at the same time. McCluskey called to his rear gunner on the intercom, but there was no answer. Despite the pain in his shoulder, McCluskey turned around. Chochalousek was still manning his machine gun, but the need was now less urgent. He had shot down one Zero, and the other soon turned tail. For a man barely out of gunnery school, Chochalousek had acquitted himself well.

But McCluskey's problems were not yet over. When he reached the point where the *Enterprise* and the *Hornet* were supposed to recover their planes, the carriers were not there. They had been slowed down by the launching and recovery of combat patrol planes, and were still 60 miles away to the northeast. No one had informed McCluskey or the other fliers that the carriers were behind schedule, and many of them were dangerously low on fuel. McCluskey scouted in a circle, and finally spotted a carrier. He was just about to land when he discovered it was the

Yorktown. Then he sighted the *Enterprise* behind it and dropped down safely. There were only two gallons of gas left in his tank.

Despite his wound, McCluskey had to consider himself lucky. Many of the pilots who had survived the attacks on the carriers had to ditch their planes in the sea when they ran out of gas. Some were rescued, others were not. The rest of the planes gradually trickled back to the carriers. The crews were shocked at the number of planes that did not return. The *Enterprise* had lost 14 dive bombers, 10 torpedo bombers, and one fighter. The *Hornet* had lost all 15 of its torpedo bombers, 12 fighters, and an undetermined—until later—number of bombers. The *Yorktown* had lost 12 torpedo bombers, two dive bombers, and three fighters.

XIV

TARGET: THE YORKTOWN

On the morning of June 4, Admiral Yamamoto and his staff aboard the battleship *Yamato*, about 450 miles west of the Japanese carrier force, were eagerly awaiting news of the Midway strike. Although radio silence was still being maintained between the Main Body and the Striking Force, the *Yamato* was picking up reports from planes in the Midway area. Yamamoto learned that a U.S. search plane had sighted the carriers, that Lt. Tomonaga had called for a second strike, and that Midway-based planes were attacking the Striking Force. Then, at 7:28, he learned that the *Tone*'s search plane had sighted a U.S. naval force.

Although Yamamoto's plan was based upon complete surprise, these developments apparently did not disturb the Admiral and his staff. On the contrary, they professed to be quite pleased. If the U.S. Pacific Fleet was already in the Midway area, then they would finish it off all the sooner. Everything was turning out just as they had wanted—the U.S. Fleet had been drawn to the Midway bait. For the next three hours, the news was reassuring. Nagumo even broke radio silence to inform Yamamoto that all attacks on his carriers had been repulsed without damage and that he (Nagumo) was now pursuing the U.S. Fleet.

Just before 10:30, the bad news started coming in. First there was a message that the *Akagi* was on fire, then the *Kaga* and the *Soryu*. Even now Admiral Yamamoto and his staff professed not to be alarmed. The damage to the three carriers probably wasn't serious, and the *Hiryu* was untouched. The battle was only beginning. But at 10:50, Yamamoto received a message that had a stunning impact. It was from Rear Admiral Hiroaki Abe on the cruiser *Tone*. Abe, who was second in command of the Striking Force, had temporarily taken charge while Nagumo was being transferred to the *Nagara*. Abe's message minced no words:

"Fires are raging aboard the *Kaga*, *Soryu*, and *Akagi* resulting from attacks carried out by land-based and carrier-based attack planes. We plan to have the *Hiryu* engage the enemy carriers. In the meantime, we are retiring temporarily to the north and assembling our forces...."

At the same time that he sent this report, Admiral Abe also sent an order to Admiral Yamaguchi on the *Hiryu*: "Attack enemy carriers."

The *Hiryu* had escaped being attacked that morning simply because it was a considerable distance away from the other carriers when the U.S. dive bombers arrived on the scene.

Admiral Yamaguchi, who had seen the smoke rising from the other carriers, wasted no time responding to Admiral Abe: "All our planes are taking off now for the purpose of destroying the enemy carriers."

Actually, Yamaguchi had only 18 Val dive bombers and six Zeros available at the moment. The Kates that had returned from the Midway strike were being rearmed with torpedoes, but there was no time to wait for them now. The six Zeros were all that could be spared. The rest would be needed to fly combat air patrol.

Admiral Yamaguchi addressed his pilots on the flight deck before they manned their planes. He told them that everything depended on them now, and warned them not to attempt anything reckless. They must remain cool, and carry out the attack with all the skill at their command. By 10:58, all 24 planes were in the air and heading for the U.S. Fleet.

The first U.S. carrier in their line of approach was the *Yorktown*. At 11:52, the *Yorktown*'s radar unit picked up the Japanese flight and reported to Admiral Fletcher, "Bogeys, 32 miles, closing." The air-raid alarm began sounding at once, and frantic preparations got underway to repel the attack. The *Yorktown*'s combat air patrol of 12 Wildcat fighters, which had been circling overhead, was ordered out to intercept the attackers. Commander Maxwell Leslie's dive bombers, which had returned from the strike on the *Soryu* and were waiting overhead to land, were waved away. Fuel lines were drained and filled with carbon dioxide, fire-fighting crews were at their posts, and all antiaircraft guns were manned. The *Yorktown* began maneuvering radically to make itself a more difficult target. Meanwhile, the *Yorktown*'s screening force of cruisers and destroyers closed around to protect the carrier.

The Japanese attack group couldn't miss finding the U.S. Fleet. The air was filled with American planes returning to their carriers from the strikes against Nagumo's force. The Japanese planes just followed them in. The temptation to pounce on some U.S. bombers proved too much for the Zeros, however. They swooped down on a group of dive bombers and got more than they bargained for. Two of the Zeros were shot up so badly they had to return to the *Hiryu*. Now there were only four Zeros left to escort the Vals.

A few minutes before noon, Lt. Michio Kobayashi, the leader of the dive-bomber group, sighted a U.S. carrier (the *Yorktown*) about 30 miles ahead. "Form up for attack," he ordered. Suddenly, without warning, 12 Wildcat fighters jumped his group from above. Almost at once, several Vals burst into flames and began plunging into the sea. The Wildcats swarmed all over the formation, but eight of the Vals managed to get through.

Now the antiaircraft gunners of Task Force 17 waited until they got within range. The sky was soon full of flak, and another bomber plunged into the sea. Then the lead Val began its dive on the *Yorktown*. It was torn to pieces by antiaircraft fire, but as it disintegrated, its bomb worked free and tumbled down on the *Yorktown*'s flight deck. The explosion almost wiped out two of the antiaircraft gun crews, set fires in the hangar below, and spread heavy smoke through the ship. Fortunately, the hangar deck officer was able to open the sprinkler system, and water quickly doused the flames there.

The other Vals also dove, hurtling down to less than 1,000 feet before pulling out. A second bomb went through three decks and finally exploded deep inside the ship at the base of the stack. This bomb did extensive damage and started severe fires. The blast disabled or snuffed out all but one of the *Yorktown*'s boilers. Within 20 minutes, the ship came to a dead halt. Another bomb exploded in a rag storage compartment, setting the whole area on fire. No one was worried about the loss of rags, but right next door were the ship's magazine, where ammunition was stored, and gasoline tanks. The magazine was flooded with sea water and the tanks filled with carbon dioxide, ending the danger from that quarter.

By 12:16, the Japanese attack was over. Their remaining planes—five dive bombers and one fighter—headed back toward the *Hiryu*. On the *Yorktown*, men fought to control fires, including one that had driven Admiral Fletcher from the bridge. Repair units rushed to cover the holes in the flight deck; steel plates were set in place to make it usable again. Below, men struggled to repair the boilers so the *Yorktown* could get up steam.

The explosions and fires had knocked out most of the *Yorktown*'s communications, as well as bringing the carrier to a halt. About 12:30, Admiral Fletcher decided he could no longer direct Task Force 17 from the *Yorktown* and would transfer with his staff to the cruiser *Astoria*. Once aboard the *Astoria*, Fletcher ordered another cruiser to take the *Yorktown* in tow. This order proved unnecessary. The *Yorktown* was beginning to get up steam, and would soon make 18 knots on its own. Unfortunately, it would not be able to evade a second attack by *Hiryu* bombers that were already on the way.

Admiral Yamaguchi had been rushing preparations for a torpedo-bomber strike ever since the Val dive bombers left. So far, Japanese intelligence reports had indicated that only one U.S. carrier was in the area, but Yamaguchi doubted that very much. The large number of planes involved in the attacks on the Striking Force convinced him that a second U.S. carrier had to be in the vicinity somewhere.

At 12:45, a pilot returning from the *Yorktown* attack reported, "Enemy carrier is burning." The Japanese were elated. Now, they believed, there was only one U.S. carrier left, and they could fight it on even terms.

Their joy was short-lived, however. A few minutes later, a scout plane attached to the *Soryu* landed on the *Hiryu*'s flight deck with some startling news: At 11:30, the pilot had sighted *three* U.S. carriers. He had been unable to report his discovery because his radio wasn't working. He had flown back to the *Soryu*, found it burning, and finally reached the *Hiryu* at 12:50. This report, of course, changed the whole picture. Now the *Hiryu* had to contend with two U.S. carriers, not one, and it was evident from radio reports that the attack on the *Yorktown* had been costly.

Yamaguchi decided to attack the U.S. carriers as soon as possible with every available plane. He had 10 Kates, one of them picked up from the *Akagi*, and six Zeros, two of them picked up from the *Kaga*. The Kates were now armed for a torpedo attack. Lt. Tomonaga, who had led the Midway strike, was chosen to lead this group. It was assumed at the time that Tomonaga's left fuel tank, which was damaged during the attack on Midway, had been repaired. Soon after, Tomonaga's mechanic told him that the repairs had not yet been made. "Don't worry," Tomonaga said. "Leave the left tank as it is and fill up the other. And hurry it up. We're taking off." For Tomonaga, this was going to be a suicide mission. Even if his plane was not shot down, he would not have enough gas to return to the *Hiryu*. Other pilots offered to exchange planes with him, but Tomonaga steadfastly refused.

Once again the pilots were assembled on the flight deck and Admiral Yamaguchi addressed them. He told them that they were the last hope, and urged them to do their best for Japan. It was essential, he said, to attack the carriers that had not been hit. There would be no recognition problem: The last report had described the damaged U.S. carrier as "burning furiously." Then Yamaguchi shook hands with Tomonaga, and thanked him for all he had done. Like everyone else, Yamaguchi knew that Tomonaga had no hope of coming back. By 1:30, the attack group was launched and heading for the U.S. Fleet.

Just after two o'clock, the *Yorktown* was making five knots, and the repair crews were confident that they would soon have enough steam to increase its speed to 20 knots. There was more good news: All the fires were under control, and it was safe to refuel the fighters then on the flight deck. Meanwhile Admiral Spruance had dispatched two cruisers and two destroyers from his own force to assist the *Yorktown*, and they were now taking up their positions. As if to celebrate the carrier's recovery, Captain Elliott Buckmaster raised a huge new American flag from the foremast. The spirits of the crew soared.

Then, at 2:10, radar picked up the second flight of enemy bombers coming in. As the ship's radio blared, "Stand by to repel attack," the *Yorktown* struggled to pick up enough speed to launch its fighters into a favorable wind. The carrier was able to send up eight Wildcats to join the four already in the air to intercept the attackers.

When the Japanese attack planes sighted the U.S. task force from a distance of 30 miles, they saw a large carrier encircled by a screen of smaller warships. The carrier was *not* "burning furiously," and appeared to be in perfect condition. The pilots were sure that this could not possibly be the same carrier their dive bombers had struck earlier. So Lt. Tomonaga ordered his torpedo bombers to form up for an attack, and once again the *Yorktown* was the target. It was now 2:32.

About 10 miles from the task force, the formation was jumped by the *Yorktown*'s fighters. This time, the Zeros provided effective cover. While the opposing fighter planes engaged in a hot battle, the torpedo bombers continued to bore in toward the carrier. Then they split up into two groups to attack the *Yorktown* from different directions. One group was led by Tomonaga, the other by Lt. Toshio Hashimoto. As they swooped down to about 150 feet above the water, the Kates ran into a hail of antiaircraft fire from every ship in the task force. The group led by Tomonaga broke up to attack singly. Hashimoto's group continued flying in a loose V-formation. Some of the Kates disintegrated as they came in, but others got through the antiaircraft fire and released their torpedoes. As one of the planes pulled out, its rear gunner shook his fist in defiance. A moment later, this plane was also destroyed.

The *Yorktown* was able to dodge the first two torpedoes, but two others struck within a half a minute of each other. Both explosions shook the carrier violently. The first ripped open fuel tanks on the port side, sending oil cascading into the sea. The second killed every man in the generator room and knocked out all power on the carrier. The *Yorktown*'s rudder jammed, the ship came to a halt, and immediately began to list.

Fortunately, the attack on the carrier was about over. It lasted just 12 minutes, and at 2:52 the remaining Japanese planes were on their way back to the *Hiryu*. Five Kates and three Zeros — half the original force — made it. Lt. Tomonaga's plane was not among the survivors. When last seen, it was heading into devastating antiaircraft fire. Lt. Hashimoto did survive, and on the way back radioed to Admiral Yamaguchi: "Two certain torpedo hits on an *Enterprise*-class carrier. Not the same one as reported bombed." Of course, Hashimoto was mistaken about that.

Within minutes after the attack ended, the *Yorktown* was listing so badly that Captain

Buckmaster ordered it abandoned. "I didn't see any sense in drowning 2,000 men just to stick with the ship," he said later. Destroyers moved in close as hundreds of men began milling about the flight deck. They were sad about losing their ship, but many tried to keep their spirits up with jokes. Soon they were descending dozens of knotted ropes cast over the starboard side. But if there were jokes, there was a grim side, too, as men learned which of their buddies had been killed or wounded. And there was astonishing heroism as well. One wounded man climbed aboard a destroyer unassisted and said, "Help some of those other poor guys who are really hurt." His own leg was severed at the knee.

The *Yorktown* proved to be almost unsinkable. It was still afloat on June 5, and was taken in tow. The next day, a large salvage crew went aboard to help keep it afloat. But that afternoon a Japanese submarine slipped through a screen of U.S. destroyers and fired four torpedoes at it. Two of the torpedoes struck the carrier, and one hit an adjacent destroyer, the *Hammann*, amidships. The destroyer sank in four minutes with a great loss of lives. The *Yorktown* was still afloat at dawn on June 7, but listing badly. The gallant ship finally went down at 6 o'clock as destroyer crews stood at attention and flags were lowered to half-mast.

XV

DEATH OF THE *HIRYU*

While the second attack on the *Yorktown* was coming in, Admiral Fletcher was following the action from the cruiser *Astoria*. Fletcher was more than a little upset. Obviously the Japanese knew where to find his carrier, but where in the Pacific was theirs? Even before the first attack, he had launched a group of scout bombers to find the undamaged Japanese carrier, but so far he had received no reports. The scout planes had been searching for more than three hours and had found nothing. But at 2:30, one of the search pilots, Lt. Samuel Adams, sighted the Japanese force as he was returning to the *Yorktown*. He carefully counted 10 ships, including a carrier, steaming north at 20 knots.

Adams radioed their position to the *Yorktown* just as the second Japanese attack was approaching the carrier. Before the *Yorktown* could relay the message via its own radio, all power on the ship failed. So the report had to be sent to the *Astoria* by blinker signal. Admiral Fletcher finally knew where the fourth Japanese carrier was, but it was too late for him to do anything about it. He relayed the information to Admiral Spruance on the *Enterprise*, and now it was up to the commander of Task Force 16 to launch an attack.

The *Enterprise* had only 11 of its own dive bombers left, but it had also picked up 14 refugee dive bombers from the *Yorktown*. All the pilots had taken part in the attack on the three Japanese carriers that morning and were thoroughly tired. Moreover, they would have to fly without fighter escort as the remaining Wildcats were needed for combat air patrol. Soon the radio blared, "Pilots, man your planes," and at 3:30 they were launching. Led by Lt. Earl Gallaher, they sped northwest toward the *Hiryu*. This time they would have no difficulties finding their target.

While these planes were launching, the crew of the *Hornet* was overjoyed by the unexpected return of 11 of its dive bombers. These were the planes that had missed the Nagumo force in the morning and had refueled at Midway. When no word was received from them, the *Hornet* assumed they had all ditched at sea. But they reappeared after three o'clock and were soon landing on the *Hornet*'s flight deck. They were immediately refueled and launched again to join the attack on the *Hiryu*. Five other *Hornet* dive bombers were sent up with them.

Lt. Hashimoto's report that a second U.S. carrier had been damaged revived hopes of victory on the *Hiryu*. Now, it was believed, the odds were one-to-one, and another strike might yet win the battle for Japan. As soon as Lt. Hashimoto returned, Yamaguchi assigned him to lead a third attack on the U.S. force.

By this time, however, Yamaguchi had very few planes left. Only five dive bombers and four torpedo bombers were still operational. A few Zeros remained, but these were needed to protect the *Hiryu*. In addition, his pilots were exhausted and the crew wasn't in much better condition. So Yamaguchi decided to defer his attack until six o'clock. At dusk, his planes would have a better chance of slipping through the enemy's defenses, and meanwhile the weary pilots and crew could rest and have a meal. No one, in fact, had eaten since breakfast.

While the meal was being served, a fast scout plane was tuned up to search for the "last" U.S. carrier. The plane was getting ready to take off when, at 5:03, a lookout shouted, "Enemy dive bombers directly overhead!" Lt. Gallaher's planes had come in with the sun behind them and, as the Japanese had no radar, their approach had not been detected.

Zeros tore at the bombers as they dove and sent three of them crashing into the sea. The *Hiryu* turned sharply to avoid the attack, but the maneuver was only briefly successful. The first bombs were near-misses, but then four direct hits were scored in succession. Columns of heavy black smoke rose from the carrier at once. The pilots knew it had been mortally wounded.

The once-proud Striking Force got very little respite for the next hour. Two of the dive bombers attacked the battleship *Haruna* before returning home. Then three separate attacks were made on the Japanese ships by B-17 bombers from Midway, and another by the *Hornet*'s dive bomber group. Miraculously, none of these attacks scored any hits.

For the *Hiryu*, it was too late for miracles. One bomb had blown off the platform of the forward elevator and sent it crashing against the bridge, blocking all forward vision from the area. The other bombs had started severe fires throughout the ship and trapped many of the men in the engine rooms. But the *Hiryu* was still making 30 knots, and there was hope that the ship might yet get clear of the battle area and U.S. planes.

Everything hinged on bringing the fires under control. Despite the staunch efforts of the crew, flames kept eating away at the ship, and some time after nine o'clock that evening the *Hiryu* came to a halt. Then the destroyer *Kazagumo* pulled alongside and sent men aboard to help fight the fires. For a while it seemed that the flames were dying down, but near midnight a great blast caused them to flare out of control again. At 2:30 A.M., Admiral Yamaguchi sent a message to Nagumo saying that he was ordering the *Hiryu*'s crew to abandon ship. The men assembled on the torn flight deck, and Admiral Yamaguchi addressed them for the last time. He told them that they were brave men and he was proud of all their past achievements. As for the loss of the *Soryu* and the *Hiryu*, which he commanded, he said, "I am fully and solely responsible.... I shall remain on board to the end." Then he gave them his final command — to continue their loyal service to the Emperor.

At 4:30, the last of the crew were transferred to destroyers. Captain Tomeo Kaku insisted upon remaining aboard with Admiral Yamaguchi, and did. At 5:10, in accordance with Yamaguchi's instructions, a destroyer fired a torpedo into the burnt-out hulk. Then the destroyer left to rejoin what was left of the Striking Force.

Somehow the *Hiryu* remained afloat for a few hours more. For approximately 50 men who had been trapped below in the engine rooms, there was an unexpectedly happy ending. The torpedo blast opened up an escape passage, enabling them to work their way up to the now-abandoned flight deck. When the *Hiryu* finally went down after nine o'clock, they put to sea in a cutter. No help arrived for 14 days, and several of the men died of exhaustion. On the 15th day, a small U.S. warship appeared and picked up the survivors, who were in no condition to argue. For these men, the war was over and they were alive.

XVI

YAMAMOTO CALLS IT OFF

The report that three of Nagumo's carriers were afire and disabled produced consternation in Admiral Yamamoto and his staff officers. The disaster was so enormous they could hardly believe it. Their earlier optimism turned to despair, and for a time all they could do was look at each other speechless. But Admiral Yamamoto soon rallied and began making plans to salvage victory from these initial setbacks.

His only hope now was to concentrate all his forces at Midway and overwhelm the U.S. Fleet by sheer weight of numbers. After ordering his own battleships to rush to the support of Nagumo's crippled carrier force, Yamamoto issued similar orders to other naval units at 12:20. Admiral Kondo, in command of the Midway Occupation Force, was already rushing north with most of his warships, having left only enough to guard the Transport Group. Admiral Kakuji Kakuta was to leave the Aleutians and hurry south with his striking force that included the light carriers *Ryujo* and *Junyo*. Two squadrons of submarines were to take up new positions at Midway.

Admiral Yamamoto still believed that the U.S. Fleet could be destroyed and Midway captured. At 1:10, he order Admiral Kondo to dispatch part of his force to "bombard and destroy enemy air bases on Midway" during the night. Kondo promptly sent four big new cruisers racing toward the island to carry out the assignment.

Admiral Yamamoto had received so many conflicting reports about the makeup of the U.S. Fleet that he had only a very confused picture of its strength. But at 4:15, Admiral Yamaguchi radioed a message that described the U.S. Fleet fairly accurately for the first time. "From our returning pilots' reports," Yamaguchi said, "the enemy force is apparently composed of three carriers, five large cruisers, and 15 destroyers." Until now, Yamamoto had believed that only one U.S. carrier was at Midway, and he was surprised to learn of the presence of two others.

But the last line of Yamaguchi's message seemed encouraging: "Our attacks succeeded in damaging two carriers." The situation wasn't so bad after all. The *Hiryu* was still intact, and when all of Yamamoto's forces arrived at Midway within a day or so, it would get better.

Admiral Nagumo, however, had been strangely silent. The last time Yamamoto had heard from him directly was at 11:50. Nagumo reported that three of his carriers were out of action, but added that he was planning to attack the enemy promptly with his "entire force." Yamamoto finally received another message from Nagumo at 5:30. It said, *"Hiryu* burning as a result of bomb hits." Once again Admiral Yamamoto and his staff were struck dumb.

What had become of Nagumo's intention to attack the U.S. Fleet head-on with all his remaining ships? On second thought, he had decided it would be quite foolhardy. With three and later four of his carriers out of action, the Americans enjoyed overwhelming air superiority. Why should they engage in an old-fashioned, surface fleet action? They would simply retire a safe distance away and make repeated air attacks on the Japanese force. As Captain Fuchida later wrote, "It was clear that however desperately we dashed ahead, there would be little chance of engaging in a successful battle. We would only be throwing ourselves into the enemy's trap."

But as commander of the Striking Force, Nagumo had to do *something*. He decided that he would have a much better chance counterattacking at night. The U.S. carriers did not then have night-flying, radar-equipped planes. (Neither did the Japanese.) That would completely neutralize U.S. air superiority. In addition, the Japanese were better trained in night-fighting tactics than the Americans. This would even out the advantage of radar units in U.S. warships. So Nagumo began preparing to attack the U.S. Fleet after dark. All destroyers that were standing by to assist the stricken carriers were summoned to rejoin the force, and the only night-scouting plane the Japanese had was made ready to search for the enemy.

Most of Nagumo's staff officers were highly skeptical about these actions. There was little chance of a single plane being able to locate the U.S. Fleet at night. And if the carriers should sink without any help at hand, what would become of their crews? As far as these officers were concerned, the battle was already lost, but no one could bring himself to suggest withdrawal openly. Probably Nagumo himself shared their view, but felt obliged to make one more effort.

Then, at 6:30, a blinker message from the cruiser *Chikuma* ended whatever hopes Nagumo still had. The message said, "At 5:13 this ship's No. 2 plane sighted four enemy carriers, six cruisers, and 15 destroyers at a point 30 miles east of the burning carrier. The enemy force is proceeding westward." This report was, of course, quite erroneous, doubling the number of U.S. carriers that were still intact. But at this point Nagumo was ready to believe almost anything about the U.S. Fleet. He didn't even bother to have the report checked. With "four" U.S. carriers steaming in his direction, his force would be wiped out. At 7:05, Nagumo decided that he had had enough. He ordered rescue destroyers to return to the disabled carriers, and the rest of his force to withdraw to the northwest as soon as possible.

Perhaps Admiral Yamamoto sensed that his commanders were losing heart. At 7:15, he radioed a message to all of them that was clearly intended to raise morale. It said:

1. The enemy fleet has been practically destroyed and is retiring eastward.

2. Combined Fleet units in the vicinity are preparing to pursue the remnants of the enemy force and, at the same time, to occupy Midway.

3. The Main Body will reach [the Midway area] at 3 A.M. on the 5th.

4. The Carrier Striking Force, Invasion Force (less Cruiser Division 7), and Submarine Force will immediately contact and attack the enemy.

Admiral Nagumo was not impressed with this heroic summons to action. At 9:30 he answered Yamamoto with a report that the U.S. Fleet now had *five* carriers and that his force was already retiring from the area. The reaction aboard the *Yamato* was predictable. "The Nagumo force has no stomach for a night engagement," Admiral Ugaki remarked. Soon afterward, Admiral Yamamoto relieved Nagumo of his command and replaced him with the aggressive Admiral Kondo. Kondo was spoiling for a night attack on the U.S. Fleet, and was rushing up north with his battleships and cruisers to carry it out. But at 11:40, the *Yamato* monitored a message from Kondo indicating there was little hope that he would find the U.S. Fleet before dawn. After dawn, of course, Kondo's ships would be at the mercy of U.S. air attacks.

Yamamoto's staff began to search desperately for ideas that might yet turn the tide of battle. But all their proposals were completely unrealistic and were treated with contempt by Admiral Ugaki. "In battle, as in chess," Ugaki said, "it is the fool who lets himself be led into a reckless move through desperation." Finally an officer protested, "But how can we apologize to His Majesty for this defeat?"

Admiral Yamamoto, who had been silent up to this time, spoke up. "Leave that to me," he said curtly. "I am the only one who must apologize to His Majesty."

Clearly Yamamoto had accepted defeat and was ready to abandon any further attempts to engage the U.S. Fleet or to capture Midway. At 12:15, he called off the plan for a night attack on the U.S. Fleet and ordered Kondo and Nagumo to join the Main Body instead. The order to bombard Midway was cancelled, and the four cruisers assigned to the mission were also ordered to join the Main Body. At 2:55, Yamamoto radioed all his commanders, "The Midway Operation is cancelled." All Japanese forces were to reassemble at a designated meeting point from which they would begin their journey back to Japan.

The Battle of Midway was practically over, but

neither Admiral Spruance, the commanders at Midway, nor Admiral Nimitz at Pearl Harbor knew it. Spruance, in fact, had to make some hard decisions on the night of June 4-5. The last of his planes from the *Hiryu* strike had been recovered shortly after seven o'clock. What should he do now? Some of his staff officers were strongly in favor of pursuing the rest of Nagumo's force and finishing it off. With all the Japanese carriers out of action, this was the perfect opportunity. Admiral Spruance wasn't so sure. Even if the Japanese had no other carriers in the vicinity, he didn't want to risk a night engagement with Yamamoto's battleships and cruisers. At night, his aircraft carriers would be highly vulnerable, and they were all the Pacific Fleet had now. To the dismay of some of his staff, Spruance decided to withdraw his task force to the east, and did not reverse his course until after midnight.

As Spruance later explained in his report to Admiral Nimitz, "I did not feel justified in risking a night encounter with possibly superior enemy forces, but on the other hand, I did not want to be too far away from Midway next morning. I wished to be in a position from which either to follow up retreating enemy forces, or to break up a landing attack on Midway...."

So during the night of June 4-5, Spruance cautiously stayed out of reach of the enemy. His decision proved to be a wise one. If he had pursued a westward course after seven o'clock, he would have run into Kondo's (and Nagumo's) force shortly after midnight. This was exactly what Yamamoto was hoping for. Then he would move in with the Main Body, and finish off the U.S. Pacific Fleet. That it never happened was due to Spruance's cool judgment.

XVII

TWO FINAL VICTIMS

On the morning of June 5, most of Yamamoto's fleet had reassembled about 320 miles northwest of Midway and was soon retiring beyond the range of Admiral Spruance's carrier planes. The four big carriers of the Striking Force were gone now, but it was still a formidable armada. Ironically, the great majority of the Japanese ships had never even fired a shot during the Battle of Midway.

While these ships were safely retiring from the Midway area, two others were experiencing serious difficulties. These were the heavy cruisers *Mogami* and *Mikuma*, two of the four that had been ordered to bombard Midway during the night of June 4-5. The four cruisers were within 90 miles of Midway when Admiral Yamamoto cancelled their mission. They then turned back, but not before they had been spotted by a U.S. submarine, the *Tambor*. The *Tambor*'s skipper, Lt. Commander John W. Murphy, radioed their presence to the U.S. Pacific Fleet command, and continued to tail them as they withdrew.

At 3:42, the *Tambor* was discovered by the Japanese force. Rear Admiral Takeo Kurita, the Japanese commander, feared a torpedo attack by the submarine, and signaled his cruisers to make a sharp turn to port. It was a difficult maneuver to execute in the dark, and it fouled up. The *Mogami* rammed into the *Mikuma* as it was turning. The *Mikuma* suffered only a ruptured oil tank, but the *Mogami*'s bow was smashed so badly that the ship could only make 12 knots. Admiral Kurita assigned his two destroyers to escort the damaged cruisers while he hurried on with the other cruisers to join the Main Body.

The *Tambor*'s message that it had sighted "many unidentified ships" was picked up by Midway's commanders, who were expecting a Japanese attack all that night. (A lone Japanese submarine did shell Midway at 1:30 A.M., but it was quickly driven off by Marine shore batteries.) The *Tambor*'s report seemed ominous, and before dawn all available Catalinas were sent up to search for the Japanese force. At 6:30, a Catalina sighted the *Mogami* and *Mikuma* about 125 miles west of Midway and reported them as "two battleships streaming oil."

The fact that the warships were retiring from Midway was a relief to the atoll, but Captain Simard wasn't about to let them off the hook. He immediately ordered an attack by his Marine bombing squadron, which now had only six Dauntless dive bombers and six Vindicators left. They took off promptly, and 45 minutes later picked up an oil slick on the ocean that led westward. They followed the slick to the two cruisers, attacking at 8:05. The dive bombers plunged first, then the Vindicators made a glide-bombing run. The cruisers' antiaircraft fire was so heavy that the planes were unable to bomb accurately and scored no hits. One Vindicator caught on fire on the way in. Its pilot, Captain Richard E. Fleming, deliberately plunged into the *Mikuma*. The crash started fires that disabled the engine room, and now the *Mikuma* was also incapable of making more than 12 knots. Both cruisers continued to plod westward at this speed.

Admiral Spruance was also on the track of the damaged cruisers. Then he began to receive search-plane reports indicating that a large Japanese force, trailed by a burning carrier, was about 200 miles to the northwest. These reports were very late in reaching Admiral Spruance, and were quite misleading. By the time Spruance received them, the *Hiryu* — the last of the Japanese carriers — had already sunk. Spruance, of course, could not know this. He felt compelled to go after the reported carrier, and this led to another wild-goose chase. His planes discovered only one Japanese ship, the destroyer *Kanikaze*, which Nagumo had sent to determine whether the *Hiryu* was still afloat. More than 50 dive bombers attacked the *Kanikaze*, but the destroyer twisted and turned and managed to elude every bomb. It even shot down the bomber piloted by Lt. Samuel Adams. So June 5th proved to be a frustrating day for Admiral Spruance and his fliers. The only damage inflicted on a Japanese ship that day was caused by Captain Fleming's crash onto the *Mikuma*.

Spruance changed course during the night, leading him back toward the *Mogami* and *Mikuma*. Before sunrise, he launched 18 scout planes to search for them. The cruisers were sighted at 6:45, and Spruance launched three separate groups of dive bombers and fighters to attack. With no Zeros to oppose them, the U.S. pilots tore into the cruisers with abandon. One plane was shot down by antiaircraft fire, but the two cruisers were soon reduced to a shambles. The *Mikuma* was abandoned and sank that night. The *Mogami* made it back to a Japanese base, but was out of action for more than a year.

At sundown, June 6, Admiral Spruance took stock of his situation. He was more than 400 miles west of Midway, his pilots were exhausted, and all his ships were low on fuel. He decided that he had pushed his luck far enough, and that further chase to the west would be too risky. Shortly after seven o'clock, he turned his ships eastward to refuel.

The Battle of Midway was over.

XVIII

WHY THE U.S. WON

The Battle of Midway changed the whole course of the war in the Pacific. It was a smashing defeat for the Japanese Navy, the first it had suffered in modern times. Although most of the fleet was still intact, the loss of four big carriers at Midway removed its offensive sting. From then on, the Japanese had to give up their ambitious plans for new conquests and assume a defensive role. As our industrial production rapidly expanded, final defeat became inevitable for Japan.

The Japanese leaders knew that Midway was a disastrous loss, but they kept it hidden from the public for years. While official radio broadcasts claimed a great victory for Japan, the carrier crews were kept in isolation, and even the wounded were not allowed to receive visitors. Soon the word went out from Imperial Headquarters that Midway was never to be mentioned.

Considering the preponderance of naval forces at Admiral Yamamoto's disposal, Midway should have resulted in the victory he so confidently expected. That it ended in a major triumph for the United States was due to many causes. Admiral Nimitz attributed the success mainly to the effectiveness of U.S. Intelligence in uncovering Yamamoto's plan even before his armada had left Japan. "Had we lacked early information of the Japanese movements," Nimitz said, "and had we been caught with our carrier forces dispersed, the Battle of Midway would have ended differently."

Early information enabled Nimitz to concentrate his forces at Midway and reduce the odds against the Pacific Fleet. But Yamamoto himself contributed a great deal to reduce the odds at Midway. His plan counted on the U.S. Fleet to react exactly as he expected, and when it didn't, the entire operation collapsed. Of what use were the powerful naval units he dispersed all over the Pacific when the U.S. task forces closed in on Nagumo's carriers at Midway? Yamamoto's plan dissipated his strength instead of concentrating it in the battle arena. And why hadn't Yamamoto delayed the Midway operation until the carriers *Shokaku* and *Zuikaku* were restored to combat service? Obviously Yamamoto completely underestimated the U.S. Pacific Fleet. His contempt for its fighting abilities stemmed from the easy victories Japan had won earlier in the war against unprepared foes. Yamamoto was a victim of "victory disease."

Admiral Spruance, who had never commanded carriers before, proved himself a superb leader.

The U.S. victory at Midway was due in large measure to his wisdom and coolness. Above all, it was due to those young aviators who never flinched when called to battle the invaders, even when they knew their chances of returning were almost nil.

BIBLIOGRAPHY

American Heritage, editors of. *Carrier War in the Pacific*. New York: American Heritage Publishing Co., Inc., 1966.

Fuchida, Mitsuo and Okumiya, Masatake. *Midway*. Annapolis: United States Naval Institute, 1955.

Lord, Walter. *Incredible Victory*. New York: Harper & Row, 1967.

Morison, Samuel Eliot. *Coral Sea, Midway and Submarine Actions*. Boston: Little, Brown and Company, 1959.

Morison, Samuel Eliot. *The Rising Sun in the Pacific*. Boston: Little, Brown and Company, 1959.

Morison, Samuel Eliot. *Two-Ocean War*. Boston: Little, Brown and Company, 1963.